B2+ Upper Intermediate

Writing

Genevieve White

Collins

HarperCollins Publishers
The News Building
1 London Bridge Street
London SE1 9GF

First edition 2014

10 9 8 7 6 5 4 3

© HarperCollins Publishers 2014

ISBN 978-0-00-754132-4

Collins® is a registered trademark of HarperCollins Publishers Limited

www.collinselt.com

A catalogue record for this book is available from the British Library

Typeset in India by Aptara

Printed and bound by CPI Group (UK) Ltd, Croydon, CR0 4YY

About the author

In 1998, an extended summer holiday led **Genevieve White** to
fall in love. The objects of her affection were a beautiful town on
the Hungarian Plain and teaching English as a foreign language.
Genevieve went on to teach in the Hungarian town of Szentes
for three years, working at a private language school and a state
secondary school. Since then she has taught in Romania, China and
various UK locations.

Genevieve is now based in the wild and windy Shetland Islands where
she teaches ESOL in a centre for community education.

CONTENTS

INTRODUCTION

English for Life: Writing B2+ will help you to develop your writing skills in everyday life.

You can use *Writing B2+* in the classroom as supplementary material for a general English course, or it is also suitable for self-study.

Using *Writing B2+*

There are two ways to use this book:

1 Work through the book from unit 1 to unit 20.
2 Look at the contents page and select the topics which are most useful or interesting to you.

Writing B2+ consists of 20 units divided into the following four sections:

- **Section 1** How am I communicating?
- **Section 2** How can I be an effective writer?
- **Section 3** What tone should I use?
- **Section 4** Who is my reader?

Unit structure

For ease of use, each unit follows a similar structure. It is recommended that you start at the beginning of the unit and work through the exercises in order. In each unit you will find the following features:

- A 'Getting started' section which introduces you to the topic of the unit.
- 'Looking closely' questions which direct your attention to a particular genre of writing, and check your understanding of it.
- 'Language focus' exercises which encourage you to look in more depth at language features of the written genre being presented.
- A 'Get writing' section which gives you the opportunity to practise what you have learned.
- A 'Next steps' section at the end of every unit provides useful suggestions for continuing to develop your writing skills in the real world.

Where appropriate there are additional pieces of information in boxes throughout the units:

- 'Language note' boxes provide extra support on writing skills and advanced language features.
- 'Useful tips' boxes provide a concise list of dos and don'ts to support you in your writing.

How to improve your writing skills

Tip 1: If you want to write well, you need to read as much as possible. Reading not only builds your vocabulary: it also develops an awareness of important features of writing such as creating tone and varying sentence structure. Read as much as you can, noting any interesting examples of language you find.

Tip 2: Practise your writing as often as you can. Working through the tasks in this book is a good start: make sure you complete the 'Next steps' tasks at the end of each unit. Don't forget to keep up the good work once you have finished this book.

Tip 3: Maintaining a blog on a topic which interests you is a very motivating way to practise writing (you can read more about this in Unit 18).

Tip 4: Revise and edit your work thoroughly, focusing first on the overall content and structure of your piece, and then on the individual sentences. Print out your work to proofread it if possible: it is much harder to spot small mistakes on a computer screen.

What is 'good' writing?

- Good writing is **clear writing**. Clear writing does not use a long sentence where a shorter one would be just as good.
- Good writing uses **appropriate word choice**. The English language is rich with synonyms: often, though, there is really only one word which will fit perfectly. Take the time to find it.
- Good writing is **audience aware**. Using an inappropriately formal or informal tone could confuse or even offend your reader. You should always reread your work once you have written it, imagining you are your reader.
- Good writing is **cohesive**. It is not a series of disconnected sentences: rather, it is a whole. Good writing moves easily through a sequence of events or a series of ideas using linking words and sentences and takes the reader with it.

Other features

At the back of the book you will find the following useful appendices:

- Useful phrases for writing formal and informal emails.
- Advice on how to lay out a formal letter.
- A list of phrasal verbs and their formal equivalents.
- Advice on proofreading your written work.
- A mini-dictionary providing definitions and example sentences for some potentially unfamiliar words in the unit. All definitions come from the *COBUILD Advanced Dictionary*.

Other titles

Also available in the *English for Life* series at B2 level: *Listening, Reading* and *Speaking*.

Available in the *English for Life* series at A2 level and B1+ level: *Writing, Speaking, Listening,* and *Reading*.

1 WRITING EMAILS
Formal, semi-formal and informal emails

Getting started

1. How many emails do you send in a week?
2. Do you usually write formal or informal emails?
3. What are some of the main differences between formal and informal emails?

Looking closely

1. Read the two emails. How well do the writers know the recipients?

Hey Marta,

How are things with you? Haven't heard from you in ages so guessing you've been busy!

Anyway, just wanted to run something past you – I'm off to London this summer for six whole weeks. ☺ This means my flat in Barcelona will be standing empty. I remember you saying something about a possible jaunt to Spain – fancy doing a bit of flat-sitting for me?

My flat is bang in the middle of town and dead handy for everything. Plus I've done it up a bit recently so it's looking nice! The public transport is awesome here, so you'd be able to get about a fair bit even without a car. What do you reckon?

Speak soon,

Katie xxx

Dear Sara,

I hope you are well and enjoying the spring sunshine.

Many thanks for contacting me about my advertisement on Flat Swap. Your flat in Edinburgh sounds as if it would be perfect. We were hoping to bring our small dog with us – do you accommodate pets?

Our flat is in the Jordaan area of Amsterdam, within easy walking distance of some wonderful shops and cafes. There's a tram stop right outside our house. I see from your Flat Swap profile that you are interested in art – are you planning to visit the Rijksmuseum?

The Jordaan is a beautiful part of a wonderful city. As I think I mentioned, our flat is in a little need of refurbishment, but I hope that this will not inconvenience you too much.

I'm really looking forward to hearing from you.

Best wishes,

Rik

Language note: formal, semi-formal and informal emails

Formal emails have formal salutations (*Dear*) and sign offs (*Kind regards*), and use fixed phrases (*I look forward to hearing from you*). There is less use of idiomatic language, and contractions are not used.

Semi-formal emails blend features of formal and informal writing. Language is neither overly colloquial nor overly formal. The tone is polite and friendly.

Informal emails have informal salutations (*Hey*) and sign offs (*Speak soon*). The language is idiomatic and has a chatty tone. Emoticons may be used, and words may be left out as long as the meaning is clear.

See Appendix 1: Useful phrases for more examples of formal and informal language.

Language focus

1 Look at the emails again. Are they formal, semi-formal or informal? Underline the words and phrases which helped you choose your answer.

2 Read Katie's email again. Rewrite these words and phrases in a more formal way.

1 I'm off to

2 bang in the middle of

3 dead handy

4 fancy … ?

5 awesome

3 Look at the phrasal verbs used in Katie's email. Rewrite these sentences in a more formal way.

1 I've done my flat up recently. ....

2 I just wanted to run something past you. ....

3 You'd be able to get about even without a car. ....

4 Read Rik's email again. Rewrite these sentences in an informal way using the phrasal verbs in the box.

check (something) out	do (something) up	be put out (by something)

1 Our flat is in need of refurbishment. ....

2 I hope this will not inconvenience you too much. ....

3 Are you planning to visit the *Rijksmuseum*? ....

Language note: phrasal verbs

We often use phrasal verbs (*do up, get about*) in informal writing, and so it is a good idea to get into the habit of using them.

However, we tend to use phrasal verbs less often in semi-formal and formal writing. Using a formal equivalent to a phrasal verb is a good way of setting an appropriately formal and serious tone.

Looking closely

1 Read the email. How well does the writer know the recipient?

Dear Dr Martin,

My colleagues and I are absolutely delighted that you have accepted our invitation to deliver a series of lectures and workshops at our university summer school in July. We are very much looking forward to working with you. Knowing your considerable subject expertise, we are sure that our students will benefit greatly from your visit.

In answer to your question, the university will provide you with accommodation for the duration of your stay. We have a flat situated close to the city centre and all its amenities; we do hope that you will find it very comfortable.

Please do not hesitate to contact me should you require any further information about your visit.

Kind regards,

Professor Cheng Li

Language focus

1 Match the extracts from the email to their functions.

1	If you require any further information please do not hesitate to contact me.	**a**	asking a question
2	I wonder if you could …	**b**	stating a reason for writing
3	With regard to …	**c**	closing expressions
4	I am writing with regard to …	**d**	referring to a point previously made.

2 Underline the formal language in the email. Then choose three of your underlined phrases and rewrite them in a less formal way. Is the meaning affected by changing the words you use?

1 ....

2 ....

3 ....

3 Read these extracts from formal emails and underline the correct answer.

1 Please do not hesitate to *contact me / give me a call* if you have any *further / more* questions.

2 I am writing *on / in* behalf of Professor Mackenzie.

3 I am writing to *enquire / ask* about …

4 I would be *grateful / delighted* if you could send me the *appropriate / right* form to *complete / fill in.*

Useful tips

- Gauge the level of formality required by reading previous emails from the person you are writing to. If none exist, err on the side of formality.
- Avoid using emoticons in semi-formal or formal emails.
- Use phrasal verbs in informal emails. Conversely, try to avoid using phrasal verbs in formal emails.
- Always check your emails carefully before you send them. You could compose your emails in a Word document before copying them into an email.

Get writing

1. Francesco is writing to an old university friend. Rewrite his email to make it less formal.

Dear Lucy,

I trust this finds you well. Please accept my apologies for the delayed response.

Thank you very much for your last email. I am planning to travel to London this autumn. Could we perhaps agree on a mutually convenient time to meet? I would appreciate it if you could alert me to any gaps in your schedule during the first week of October.

I look forward to hearing from you,

Francesco

---

2. Your elderly aunt in New Zealand emails you, inviting you to come and stay for a couple of months. Reply to her, accepting her invitation.

3. Email a close friend with an idea for a holiday you want to take together. Include descriptions of cities and places you want to visit, and suggest possible accommodation.

Next steps

Read emails you receive in English carefully. Note down useful phrases you find and try to use them in the next email you send. You could devote two sections in your notebook to phrases and language (formal and less formal) that you come across.

To find websites that focus on phrasal verbs and formal equivalents. When you learn a new phrasal verb, make sure you can express the same meaning in a more formal way.

2 WRITING LETTERS
Formal letter writing

Getting started

1 In what situations might you want to write a formal letter?
2 What are some of the main features of formal writing?
3 What is the difference between a formal letter and a formal email?

Looking closely

1 **Read the letter and answer the questions.**

1 What is the writer's purpose?
2 Why has she chosen to write a letter rather than an email?
3 Does the language used feel different to what the writer might have used in an email?
4 How is the layout different to that of an email?

---

7 Abbey Gate
Leicester
LE4 3TS

Leicester City Council
New Walk Centre
Leicester
LE1 6ZG

23 May

Dear Mayor Soulsby,

I am writing with regard to my concern about the lack of safe pedestrian walkways and cycle paths in this city. As a mother of two school-age children, I feel that the road traffic situation as it stands is extremely dangerous and should be addressed as a matter of urgency.

As I am sure you will be aware, there has been an increasing number of road accidents in the past two years. Despite the considerable amount of money which has been poured into financing road safety campaigns in schools, the situation is not improving. What needs to be remedied is the complete lack of wide pavements and dedicated cycle areas so that children (and adults) can travel to school and work safely.

I would like to request that this issue be addressed in your transport strategy. Your prompt attention to this matter would be greatly appreciated.

Yours sincerely,

A. Hassan

Ayla Hassan

Language focus

1 Read the letter again. Underline examples of the passive voice and decide why it has been used in each case.

Language note: the passive voice

We often use the passive voice in formal writing as it is less direct and therefore sounds more polite. Compare the following sentences:

Action is needed to reduce noise in residential areas.

You should act to reduce noise in residential areas.

2 Are these passive sentences correct or incorrect? Correct them if necessary.

1 Noise needs being reduced in residential areas after midnight.

2 I narrowly avoided to be run down on my way home from work last night.

3 Care should be taken to prevent further tragedies from happening.

4 Your presence at the meeting would be greatly appreciate.

Language note: intensifiers

Intensifiers make adjectives or adverbs stronger, e.g. *I'm **absolutely** exhausted.* But be careful – if you use too many intensifiers in your writing you will take away from the effect of your letter.

3 Underline the intensifiers in the letter on page 12.

4 Read these extracts from formal letters and underline the correct intensifier.

1 I am *extremely / highly* sorry to tell you that your application has been unsuccessful.

2 It is *totally / deeply* disturbing that so little has been done to rectify matters.

3 I am *most / very* eager to meet the rest of the team.

4 This has come as a *real / great* shock to me, as I have always admired your newspaper.

5 It is *really / highly* unlikely that I will visit your restaurant again.

Looking closely

1 Read the letter on page 14 and answer the questions.

1 What is the writer's purpose?

2 Why has she chosen to write a letter rather than an email?

3 Is this letter more or less formal than the letter on page 12?

4 List four words or phrases which led you to your decision for question 3.

....

....

Dear Mr Giuliani,

I am writing to inform you that I will be resigning from my post as Human Resources Manager. My last day of work will be June 28th.

I would like to thank you for giving me the opportunity to work in this department. While being excited about my move, I am deeply sorry to leave behind colleagues from whom I have learned so much. Please accept my sincere thanks for the patience and time you have invested in me.

Yours sincerely,

M. morris

Maria Morris

Language focus

1 We often use the preposition + *-ing* pattern to avoid repeating the subject of a sentence. Underline an example of this in Maria's letter.

2 Rewrite these sentences so that they follow the preposition + *-ing* pattern. The first word has been given.

    1 I understand your reasons for leaving but I am very sorry to see you go.

      While ....

    2 I made sure that I had done sufficient reading before I wrote the report.

      Before ....

    3 I made a great career decision when I chose to work at this company.

      In ....

    4 I am hoping to raise awareness of this situation so I am writing to you.

      By ....

3 Underline the fixed formal phrases in Maria's letter.

4 Read these fixed formal phrases. In each case, one word is incorrect. Rewrite the fixed phrase with the correct word.

    1 I would be grateful for a reply at your earliest convenient …

    ....

    2 I am writing to expend my concern about …

    ....

    3 I am writing in relative to …

    ....

    4 Thank you for your time and consternation …

    ....

5 When writing formal letters we often use longer, more complex sentences than we do in more informal writing. Read this letter to a newspaper. Use more complex sentences to make it more formal.

Dear Editor,

I am writing to complain about the article featured in last Friday's paper. I do not agree with S Thornton's opinions. In my opinion she is wrong. It is not just sugary food which makes our children obese and unhealthy. It is their lifestyle. I am not against modern technology at all. Yet children spend far too long on their computers. Also, they are not out in the fresh air often enough. This is not just due to our damp and cold climate. It is because of media attempts to create a climate of fear. Parents are afraid to allow their children to play outside.

W. Thomas

Useful tips

- Follow the conventions of formal letter layout (see *Appendix 2*).
- Find out the name of the person you are writing to – *Sir or Madam* is just about acceptable, but it is not ideal (it can make you look as if you haven't tried hard enough.)
- Make sure you know why you are writing the letter and get straight to the point.
- Learn some useful formal phrases from *Appendix 1: Useful phrases*. These can be used again and again to express particular sentiments in formal situations.
- Proofread your letter – are all of your fixed expressions accurate?

Get writing

1 You have recently been on an exchange trip to Japan. Write a thank-you letter to the person who showed you around, enclosing a small gift and photos of your trip.

2 Write a letter to a hotel you have stayed in, complimenting them on their wonderful service, and enclosing a postcard of your home town.

3 Write a letter to your town mayor in which you highlight a particular local issue and ask your mayor to do something about it.

Next steps

Find a website which has sample formal letters for you to study. Next time you need to write a formal letter, see if you can find a sample online to help you.

3 WRITING ONLINE (1)
Contributing to a discussion forum

Getting started

1 Online forums can be used to exchange information, to get advice and to debate issues. Can you think of examples of these types of forums?

2 Have you ever taken part in an online forum?

3 How reliable is the advice given in online forums?

Looking closely

1 **Read Stefano's post on an online travel forum. What is his problem?**

  a He doesn't have enough money.

  b He isn't sure how best to plan his trip.

2 **How formal is this discussion?**

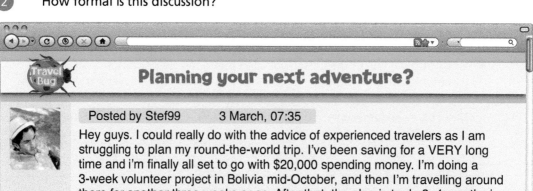

Planning your next adventure?

Posted by Stef99   3 March, 07:35

Hey guys. I could really do with the advice of experienced travelers as I am struggling to plan my round-the-world trip. I've been saving for a VERY long time and i'm finally all set to go with $20,000 spending money. I'm doing a 3-week volunteer project in Bolivia mid-October, and then I'm travelling around there for another three weeks or so. After that, the plan is to do 3–4 months in South East Asia. This leaves 6.5 months for the rest of my trip – Australia, New Zealand and Africa are all possibilities, but I don't know where to start! I thought about maybe picking up a job in New Zealand for a few weeks.
All suggestions welcome!

Reply by Nelly 4   4 March, 14:03

Personally, I would spend a few months in South America. It seems a waste to just see one country. You could look at doing something like Bolivia to Patagonia overland.

Reply by FishMD   4 March, 18:09

I would skip New Zealand (unless you have a specific reason for visiting). It tends to be difficult to find work there and it can be an expensive country. Even assuming you find a job, you'll have to factor in accommodation, food and all the rest. I agree with Nelly – you could quite possibly spend a year in South America alone!

Language focus

1 Match the informal words and phrases to their formal alternatives.

1	I could really do with	**a**	avoid
2	picking up a job	**b**	I would benefit from
3	food for thought	**c**	finding employment
4	skip	**d**	ideas to consider

2 Read these sentences from the discussion. What effect do the underlined words have on the overall meaning of the sentences?

1 It <u>seems</u> a waste to just see one country.

2 You <u>could</u> look at doing something like Bolivia to Patagonia overland.

3 It <u>tends</u> to be difficult to find work there …

4 You <u>could quite possibly</u> spend a year in South America alone!

Language note: hedging language

When giving advice, writers often use hedging language to sound more polite and less bossy. The underlined words in Exercise 2 are all examples of hedging language.

3 Read these sentences and underline the correct answer.

1 Cuba *tends to be / seems to be* fast becoming the most popular destination for young backpackers.

2 Travelling with young children can be *somehow / somewhat* stressful.

3 It *mustn't / couldn't* have been easy to save up all that money for your trip.

4 It *may well / should* be wise to spend longer in one place.

4 Rewrite these sentences. Use hedging language to make them sound more polite.

1 It's pointless going to Australia for four weeks. Either spend more time there or scrap it completely.

2 Volunteer tourism is very controversial, you know. Many people agree that it does more harm than good – you should do some research before agreeing to volunteer.

3 If you've already been to Brazil, go somewhere new instead. What's the point in spending all of your money on doing the same thing twice?

Looking closely

1 Read the community forum on page 18 and choose the best title.

a Dogs need more exercise

b Scared of dogs – help!

c Dogs in parks: proposed restrictions

2　What bill is being proposed? Why is the bill being proposed?

Posted by Tom K **on 14 February at 22:32**

Are people aware that a bill is being proposed to enforce dog owners to keep their dogs on a lead at all times in certain local parks? Responsible dog owners will be penalized for the actions of irresponsible dog owners. We need to be vigilant that this doesn't go through.

▶ Reply

Reply by Xavier **on 14 February at 22:50**

Well, who are the responsible dog owners exactly? I got bitten by a dog at Inverboyne Park a few months ago, thanks to a dog owner being unable to control the excited animal.

▶ Reply

Reply by Betty M **on 14 February at 23:11**

As a responsible parent who is sick and tired of dogs running up and barking, sniffing, chasing and trying to bite my two year old, I would like to ask what on earth is wrong with the odd dog-free park? I think it is a wonderful idea. Imagine, if you will, a park where children can run around, explore, climb, jump and play free from any form of canine intimidation.

▶ Reply

Reply by Tom K **on 14 February at 23:32**

I'm very sorry to hear that dogs are constantly trying to bite your two year old. That must be very distressing for you and your child and I sympathize with you. Dog attacks are, however, very rare and fortunately I have never seen one. Dogs which are well-behaved and good-natured shouldn't suffer because of some sort of collective vendetta against dogs in parks.

▶ Reply

Language focus

1 Is the community forum more or less formal than the travel forum? Underline the words and phrases which helped you choose your answer.

2 Read the community forum again and underline ways that the posts give the information in 1–4 below.

1 identify themselves and their own interests

2 acknowledge someone else's point of view before making their own case

3 give an example to back up their own point of view

4 ask questions to make their point

Useful tips

- When asking for advice in an opening post, include a little information about yourself so that people can advise you better. Then read all the posts carefully before you add your own reply.

- If you wrote the opening post, then it is polite to write a new post thanking people for their advice and suggestions.

Get writing

1 Imagine you are in each of these situations. Write an opening post on an online discussion forum and ask for advice.

1 You are going to Brazil and you want some travel advice about the best places to see.

2 You are getting married and need advice on planning a wedding on a tight budget.

2 Write a reply to these opening posts.

The holidays are coming and I'm getting into a right state! My five-year-old son is impossible to entertain and spends the weekends complaining about being bored! He hates staying at home, but we live miles from anywhere and he has no brothers and sisters to keep him amused. Any suggestions gratefully received!

I've been learning English for seven years and I have just completed an upper-intermediate course. Unfortunately, the language school I go to doesn't offer advanced level courses, so I'll need to continue learning English alone. Does anyone have any good tips/suggestions for ways I can continue to improve my English? Many thanks in advance for your help.

Next steps

You can participate in an online discussion forum today! Have a look for forums where:

travellers offer each other tips and advice.

learners of English discuss strategies for language learning and support each other.

participants discuss books they have enjoyed.

4 WRITING ONLINE (2) Commenting on a blog or online newspaper

Getting started

1 Do you read the news online? Have you ever commented on an article you have read?
2 Why do people comment on blogs?
3 Do people comment on online news articles for similar reasons?

Looking closely

1 Read the comments posted on an article from *The Wall Street Journal*. Choose the best title for the article.

a The dangers of smartphone addiction
b Rise of smartphone use leads to depression
c Why aren't smartphones making us more productive?

10 hours ago **Jennifer Owens** wrote:
We choose to use these wonderful devices to pursue trivial, personal and inane interests – following celebrity Twitter feeds, checking social media constantly, staring at YouTube videos, annoying everyone around us because we can't be unconnected long enough to simply shop for groceries without blabbering away on our cell phones. We use them while we're at work, in the car, on the train, at the dinner table, walking, babysitting, driving, in class, etc. – 24/7.

Recommend

8 hours ago **Suva Crew** replied:
It is a prop to avoid actually being social. Then it is also an appliance that is making us ill with overwhelming amounts of data dump we can't process. Just ask all of the moms staring at the screens in their cars, moments after popping anti anxiety pills. It catches files, it pushes files, but there is little manipulation and editing capability ... thus no value added productivity. Ever try to read a red lined contract on a smartphone?

Recommend

8 hours ago **Rocket Surgeon** replied:
I read this article. It took twice as long as it would on my laptop or desktop because the phone kept "wigging out" and reverting back to the home page. Phones and tablets cannot utilize the software that industry depends on as efficiently as a laptop, and a laptop is not as efficient as a desktop. We know why people are not more productive ... smartphones are an email retrieving device for business and nothing more IMHO.

Recommend

3 hours ago **Cameron Miller** replied:
The smartphone is a modern version of Rubik's cube ... it's there to waste time. These gizmos aren't getting people to work smarter or faster, just the opposite.

Recommend

Language focus

1 Good writers use a range of techniques to support their ideas. Read the comments again and answer the questions.

1 Who asks a rhetorical question?

2 Who backs up their opinion with their own experience?

3 Who refers back to another writer's argument and adds an idea of their own?

4 Who backs up their argument with examples from the world around them? (2 answers)

2 Rewrite this comment to make it sound more knowledgeable, less formal and less repetitive.

> We choose to use these wonderful devices to pursue trivial, personal and inane interests – following celebrity Twitter feeds, checking social media constantly, staring at YouTube videos, annoying everyone around us because we can't be unconnected long enough to simply shop for groceries without blabbering away on our cell phones. We use them while we're at work, in the car, on the train, at the dinner table, walking, babysitting, driving, in class, etc. – 24/7.

Language note: connotation

The term *connotation* refers to the cultural and emotional associations which different words carry. For example, *old* describes something which is not new. However, the word *old* also carries with it certain connotations, which vary depending on context. *Old buildings* might suggest damp and disrepair to some readers while others associate them with interesting architecture and period features.

3 Look at the different ways in which the writers refer to smartphones. Match the word to its connotations.

1 wonderful devices

2 prop

3 modern version of a rubik's cube

4 gizmos

a The writer thinks smartphones support people who can't cope with everyday life.

b The writer thinks smartphones have fantastic potential.

c The writer thinks that smartphones are enjoyable distractions, but ultimately timewasters.

d The writer thinks that smartphones are just one of a range of confusing technological gimmicks.

Looking closely

1 Read the comments from page 22 posted on a travel blog. Choose the best title for the blog post.

a Helping the tourism industry to grow

b Why tourists should stay home more often

c Why tourism is great for developing countries

2   Do you agree with the comments? Explain why or why not.

Sun worshipper

It cuts both ways. Travelling is such a great way of learning about new cultures and different ways of life.
It brings money into poorer countries too.

Wandering Will

You're absolutely right to point out the financial benefits of tourism, but the extra money and opportunities it offers should outweigh the environmental damage caused.
Right now, I'm not convinced this is the case.

Lara

Awesome post, Will! I think I'm with Sun worshipper – tourism is a mixed bag, isn't it? I guess it's all part and parcel of belonging to a global society. We have our freedom and with that freedom come responsibilities. Hmm.

Freewheeler

I agree with you, Lara – we do have responsibilities and we need to face up to them before it's too late. With too many travellers it's just take, take, take and no give. As a society we need to change our attitude to travel. We are so privileged to be able to experience different cultures and landscapes – we need to prove we are worthy of this privilege through making sustainable travel choices. Thanks, Will, for another thought-provoking post.

Language focus

1   Match the expressions from the comments to their definitions.

1	cuts both ways	**a**	something made up of different (both positive and negative) elements
2	a mixed bag	**b**	something which is necessary and cannot be avoided
3	part and parcel of	**c**	has two different effects at the same time

Language note: seeing both sides of the argument

When expressing your opinion, it is very important to show that you can see both sides of the argument and not just your own. For example, Wandering Will writes *You're absolutely right to point out the financial benefits of tourism, but the extra money and opportunities it offers should outweigh the environmental damage caused.* Readers are more likely to respect your opinion if they can see that you have considered different points of view.

2 Choose the correct word in these sentences.

1 *While / When* many tour operators are now environmentally minded, there remain many who only care about money.

2 Tourism creates jobs for many people. *However / Moreover*, it also has serious environmental consequences.

3 *Admittedly / Admitting*, many countries rely on tourism to generate income. *Yet / So* we cannot deny the stark environmental consequences of global tourism.

3 Rewrite this comment so that it acknowledges both sides of the argument.

> Tourism is great for the economy in these times of global financial insecurity. We need to do all we can to encourage it. Tourism certainly should not be halted just because of a few environmental worries.

Useful tips

- Try to write a comment which adds something new to the debate. Avoid simply repeating what has already been said.
- Feel free to start a debate as long as you can back your opinion up and acknowledge the other side of the argument.
- Vary the language you use to intensify your argument and avoid repetition.

Get writing

1 Read this comment on the rise of teenage smartphone addiction. Write a polite response, making sure to include your own point of view.

> Smartphones are the scourge of modern day life. I have three teenage daughters. All three of them have been begging me for their own smartphones since they were twelve, but I have not given in yet! If you ask me, these moronic machines are to blame for much of today's societal ills: obesity, bullying, depression … I'd throw them all in the bin!

2 You have just read a travel blog in which some very uncomplimentary things have been written about your city – the blogger has described it as ugly, dirty and unwelcoming. You are deeply offended, and would like to set the record straight for other visitors to the blog. Write a comment.

Next steps

Read a story which interests you on an online newspaper, and add your own comment to the discussion.

Next time you find useful or interesting information on a blog, write a comment to thank the writer. Remember to say why you liked the post, and what was useful about it.

5 PLANNING
Writing a reference

Getting started

1 What is a reference and when might you be asked to write one?

2 List the information which should be included in a reference.

3 Why should a written reference be formal?

Looking closely

1 Read the reference and answer the questions.

1 How do Dr Rae and Isobel know one another?

2 What job is Isobel applying for? How do you know?

Dear Mr Williamson,

1 I taught Isobel on a number of occasions during her Masters degree in English at Appalachian State University and I have a very high opinion of her academic and personal qualities.

2 She graduated in the top 5% of her class, a result which reflected her remarkably consistent standard of work: nearly half of her grades were the best in the class and most of the remainder were top 10%. She is a most conscientious and motivated student, highly organized and utterly reliable, with a confident, thoughtful and cheerful personality which made her a most welcome member of any tutorial. Her commitment to her studies is obvious and I have not the slightest doubt that she will successfully complete her postgraduate teaching course and make a very valuable contribution to her chosen career.

3 Isobel has great experience of teaching. My department employed her in her final year as one of the five tutors on our access course (aimed primarily at adult learners wishing to return to education). I was closely involved in the selection process and I can happily disclose that Isobel was the first choice for the position out of all of those we interviewed. Isobel was also accepted onto the JET scheme for teaching English in Japan. This is a highly prestigious program with fierce competition for places and only personal circumstances obligated her to decline the opportunity.

4 It is a pleasure to support Isobel's application unreservedly. Should you require any further information please do not hesitate to contact me.

Yours sincerely,

S.Rae

Dr Sarah Rae

Language note: writing a reference

References should avoid slang, colloquialisms, informal language and refrain from making jokes. Do not include negative remarks about the candidate, or information about their marital status, appearance, age, religious beliefs or political affiliations. Ask yourself what your reader wants to know and make sure that you address any questions they may have.

Language focus

1 Read the reference again. What is the purpose of paragraphs 1–4?

2 Look at this plan for writing a reference. Number the information in the correct order.

a concrete information about the candidate's achievements ....

b the dates the candidate was employed by you or working with you ....

c the candidate's current job title ....

d exceptional qualities which the candidate possesses ....

e information about your position ....

3 Here are some questions the reader of the reference might have. Read the reference and underline the answers.

1 How academically able is the candidate?

2 Does the candidate have good interpersonal skills?

3 How diligent is the candidate?

4 What relevant experience does the candidate have?

5 How does the writer know the candidate?

4 Circle the character adjectives in the reference.

5 Look at the character adjectives in the box and read the situations below. For each situation, choose four character adjectives which you would include in your reference.

creative	resourceful	dedicated	competitive	caring	dynamic
mature	innovative	focused	articulate	thoughtful	conscientious

1 Your 19-year-old neighbour wants to work as an au pair abroad. She requires a character reference.

....

2 One of your students is applying to study French literature at university.

....

3 Your colleague has applied for a PR and marketing job.

....

Looking closely

1 Read the two references and answer the questions.

1 What is missing?

2 What should be removed?

Sergio is utterly caring and conscientious. I am sure that he will make a wonderful au pair, as he is wonderfully resourceful, kind and creative. He has a natural way with children, and although he can look a little dishevelled at times, is generally a personable and smart young man.

I am more than happy to support his application. Should you require any further information, please do not hesitate to contact me.

I am writing to recommend Vanessa Pia for employment. Vanessa has worked in the accounts department of *The Northman* newspaper since 2011. She was responsible for providing office support to her colleagues, including scheduling appointments, writing emails and making telephone calls.

Vanessa is an energetic and lively person who does great work for the local socialist party outside of work, and yet still manages to keep on top of all tasks assigned to her.

Vanessa's work was consistently of a very high standard, and I am more than happy to recommend her. Should you have any other questions with regard to Vanessa's qualifications or experience, please do not hesitate to contact me.

2 Write two or three sentences to:

1 describe how the writer knows Sergio.

2 support the writer's claims about Sergio with specific examples.

3 give information about Vanessa's specific achievements.

Language focus

1 Read the reference and number the paragraphs in the correct order.

a Julia would bring professionalism and competence of the highest degree to any workplace and I commend her to you wholeheartedly. Should you require any further information please do not hesitate to contact me at this address.

b I am writing to support Julia Manson's application for the post of summer tour guide with Isis tours. I had the pleasure of employing Julia for summer work between 2010 and 2013, and am delighted to have the opportunity to support her application unreservedly.

c Over the years I have known her, Julia's demeanour, dedication and attention to detail have never failed to impress me. Her natural flair for languages and her excellent communication skills made her an asset to the tourist office during the summers she worked here.

2 Paragraph d is missing. Write it using the information below.

Julia won the medal for good customer service last year.

Julia was regularly commended in customer feedback surveys conducted by the Tourist Office.

Julia recently embarked on a degree course in modern languages.

Useful tips

- Before you start writing your reference, gather together the information you will need when you are writing, e.g. the candidate's C V, the job specification (if available), academic grades, essays and examples of work.
- Think about the person you are writing about. What do you know about them? How does this match the specifications of the job they are applying for?
- It might be useful to discuss the reference with the candidate before you write it, to ensure that what you write is targeted to the specifications of the job.

Get writing

1 You are the manager of a busy coffee shop. A part-time member of staff (who is a first year English student) asks you to write a reference in support of her application to work in the city's tourist office.

2 You are a high school teacher. One of your final year students wishes to study nursing at college and asks you to write a reference. Remember to refer to his academic track record.

3 You are head of accounts at an accountancy firm. Your PA has decided to spend a year doing volunteer teaching in Mali, and asks you to write her a reference.

Next steps

Have a look for websites which have sample references. Read them and note down any expressions you find which are not included in this unit.

Visit an online recruitment site, and look at the character adjectives which are used in job advertisements. Select an advertisement. Think of someone you know well. What concrete examples can you provide to prove that they have these qualities?

6 STRUCTURING
Writing a covering letter

Getting started

1 List the differences between a CV and a covering letter.
2 How long should a covering letter be? What information should it include?
3 Have you ever written a covering letter?

Looking closely

1 Read the letter and answer the questions.

1 What position is Klaus applying for?
2 What are the job requirements of this position?

Dear Ms Heller,

1 I am writing in reply to the advertisement on your website for the post of intern journalist at Wave magazine.

2 Since discovering Wave in my first year of university I have been an avid reader. I have always admired the range of contemporary topics your writers cover, and I would welcome the opportunity to hone my own writing skills in such a dynamic and innovative environment.

3 As my CV illustrates, writing plays is a very important part in my life. Over the past few years, I have contributed articles to a range of online and print magazines. In addition to my role as editor of the university's weekly online magazine, I regularly maintain my own blog, which won the 'Student Times Blog of the Month' prize last year. Through combining writing with studies and part-time employment I have developed important skills required by this position; I am adept at organizing my time and used to meeting deadlines. Finally, I believe I possess adaptability and resourcefulness; during my exchange year in Helsinki I I learned Finnish and participated fully in the life of the local community. I would, therefore, relish the challenge of relocating to New York.

4 Thank you for your time in reading this letter. I look forward to hearing from you.

Yours sincerely,

K. Bergen

Klaus Bergen

Language focus

1 **Match paragraphs 1–4 to two pieces of information.**

a thanking the employer for their time ....

b saying why you are interested in the job ....

c complimentary close ....

d saying where you saw the position advertised ....

e referring to your attached CV ....

f stating your skills and providing concrete examples ....

g saying what position you are applying for ....

h mentioning what you know about the company ....

2 **Underline the verbs in the letter. Are they active or passive?**

3 **Read these sentence pairs. Choose the sentence which sounds best and give a reason for your choice.**

1 **a** I regularly contribute to professional journals.

   b My articles are regularly published in professional journals.

2 **a** Staff meetings were chaired by me and a colleague.

   b I co-chaired staff meetings.

3 **a** I collaborated with a colleague on a new workplace initiative.

   b I was selected to collaborate with a colleague on a new workplace initiative.

4 **a** I increased sales by 75 per cent.

   b Sales were increased by 75 per cent.

Language note: sentence structure

It can be difficult to avoid starting every sentence with 'I' when you are writing about yourself. However, it's important to vary the ways in which you begin your sentences to avoid sounding big-headed.

I have always enjoyed writing → Writing plays an important part in my life.

I possess the skills required → What is more; I believe I possess the skills required.

I discovered Freedom magazine in my first year of university → Since discovering Freedom magazine in my first year of university, I have been an avid reader.

---

4 **Rewrite the following sentences so that they don't start with 'I'. Try to make each one sound different.**

1 I have wanted to be a newspaper journalist since I was at high school.

2 I have worked in five different retail environments and have learned new skills in each one.

3 I believe in the power of qualifications but I also believe that those who work hard will be rewarded for their efforts.

4 I haven't been working in an office for long but the experiences I have had have been varied and extremely useful.

Looking closely

1 Read these extracts from two covering letters. Do you think the applicants were successful?

Text A

> I have never had any work published, but when I read through the person specification for the job I realized that I do, in fact, possess a number of the skills you require. Not only am I extremely creative, I am also a great communicator and possess exceptional organizational skills.
>
> I did start a blog once. A lot of my friends really enjoyed it, and my uncle told me I should probably be a writer!

Text B

> I am really interested in being employed by your company, as your online magazine has always appealed to me. I have always loved writing and my work has been published on online travel sites and also in the local newspaper.
>
> I feel I meet the criteria listed in the job specification. I have an extremely strong academic record, and I have managed to combine my studies with a range of other interests. I am also shrewd, creative, focused, dynamic, intelligent and unflaggingly hardworking.

Language focus

1 Read the letters again and write a tick in the correct column. There may be more than one possible answer.

		Text A	Text B
1	Which letter sounds egocentric?	....	....
2	Which letter focuses on what the writer has *not* done?	....	....
3	Which letter includes irrelevant information?	....	....
4	Which letter includes many positive qualities, but does not back these up with evidence?	....	....
5	Which letter uses the passive voice where the active voice would be better?	....	....

2 Rewrite Text B. Focus on varying the way you begin your sentences.

Useful tips

- Covering letters should be concise – one page should be the maximum length.
- Write your covering letter with the job advertisement beside you. Does your letter address all the points required? Every covering letter must be specifically tailored to fit the job for which you are applying.
- Always end your cover letter positively and look forward to the next stage. For example, *I look forward to hearing from you.*
- Refer to *Appendix 1: Useful phrases* to make sure that you are using appropriate formal language.

Get writing

1 Read the recruitment advertisements and write plans for covering letters. What information would you include? How would you address the job requirements?

International Sales Director	Overseas Representative
We are currently seeking to recruit a dynamic sales leader with a proven track record of success within the domain of computer sales. Required:	We are looking for overseas representatives to work over the summer season at our European holiday resorts. Platypus Holidays is a leading independent tour operator, and as one of our holiday representatives you will be directly responsible for ensuring the comfort and satisfaction of our guests.
▸ the ability to develop new business opportunities in a fast moving international environment	You will:
▸ a strong background within the IT industry	▸ have a working knowledge of French, German or Italian
▸ first class communication skills	▸ possess excellent social skills and a lively, positive disposition
▸ educated to degree level or equivalent	▸ be a team player
▸ proven leadership experience	▸ have experience of working in a customer service environment
This role entails a significant amount of international travel and offers the successful candidate the opportunity to play a significant part in the future success of the business.	▸ be in possession of a clean driving licence

2 Choose one of the jobs and write a covering letter.

Next steps

Visit an online recruitment site and choose a job which interests you. Read the job specification and note down ways in which your skills and experience match the requirements.

You can find examples of good (and bad) sample covering letters online. Read some sample letters and note down useful language and mistakes you should avoid making.

7 DEVELOPING
Writing an opinion piece

Getting started

1 What is an opinion piece?

2 Where can you find examples of this kind of writing?

3 Think of an opinion piece you have read recently. Was it successful and if so, why?

Looking closely

1 **Read the extract from an opinion piece. Which statement best reflects the author's opinion? Do you agree with her point of view?**

a Mothers should spend less time on their careers and more time supporting their children.

b Society puts too much pressure on mothers to spend a lot of time with their children.

'Lean In' and the era of the inconvenienced mom

by Leonore Skenazy

1 'Lean In,' says Sheryl Sandberg in her new book by that name. As chief operating officer of Facebook, she is encouraging working women not to 'push back' from their careers. Too often, she says, women fear that if they climb too high at the office, they won't have enough time for their children. Why does the worry loom so large? Blame the modern-day, mom-guilting belief that being a good mother means devoting every waking moment (give or take 30 minutes for yoga or Pinterest) to child-rearing.

2 Thanks to that delusion, college-educated mothers are spending more time with their kids than ever: an extra nine hours a week since 1995, according to a University of California at San Diego study. That's the equivalent of an entire extra workday women spend as their children's soccer-watchers, snack-selecters, flashcard-flashers, all-seven-volumes-of-Harry-Potter readers, college-essay editors and Candy-yland rivals (not necessarily in that order).

3 But in truth, both generations benefit when parents do a little more leaning out of their children's lives. Intensive parenting is coming under increasing scrutiny, and the results are so bad, pretty soon high-school seniors are going to be writing essays about the hardships they endured as helicoptered kids.

4 Helicopter-parented children tend to be sadder, fatter and less resilient than kids given more independence. A 2011 North Carolina State University study found that children play less actively when their (loving, worried) parents hover over them, even as another study, at the University of Missouri published this winter, found that the more time spent by mothers directing their children's play – do this! try that! – the more 'negative emotion' is displayed by the little ingrates.

5 By the time these cosseted kids reach college, they're ready to give up – or so concludes another study, this one by Holly Schiffrin at the University of Mary Washington in Virginia: 'Students who reported having over-controlling parents reported significantly higher levels of depression and less satisfaction with life.'

From: *The Wall Street Journal*

Language focus

1 Read the opinion piece again. Identify in which paragraph 1–5 the author does the following:

1 places the argument in its current societal context ....

2 provides anecdotal evidence to support her argument ....

3 provides research evidence to support her argument ....

4 identifies and focuses on the main argument ....

Language note: lexical fields

The writer uses the phrase *helicopter parenting* to refer to parents who stay very close to their children – in her opinion they 'hover' around like helicopters. She uses a range of words to describe a particular approach to parenting, e.g. *intensive, directing, over-controlling* and *kid-centric*.

In a good opinion piece, writers persuade the reader to share their opinions. Writers can strengthen their arguments by using words which are closely related but not the same. This makes their writing less repetitive and more interesting.

---

2 Underline the words in the text which refer to parenting. Then make a list of the words which describe 'helicopter parenting' and its effects.

3 Match the word to its definition and example. Add two examples of your own for each word.

1	synonyms	**a**	two words which occur together very often, e.g. *strong wind*
2	connotations	**b**	two words which have an opposite meaning, e.g. *strong* and *weak*
3	antonyms	**c**	words which share a thematic relationship, e.g. *parent, child, bring up, nurture, family*
4	lexical field	**d**	two words which have the same meaning, e.g. *beautiful* and *pretty*
5	collocations	**e**	the associations evoked by words which share the same basic meaning, e.g. *plump* and *overweight*.

4 Opinion piece writers often use different terms to refer to one thing. Match the underlined words to the ways in which they could be referred to in an opinion piece. Add two more ways you could refer to these objects.

1	The dangers of smoking <u>cigarettes</u>	**a**	the goggle box
2	The devastating effect of <u>cars</u> on our planet	**b**	gas guzzlers
3	Why watching <u>television</u> is such a waste of time	**c**	cancer sticks

5   Complete the extract from an opinion piece using the words in the box.

tender	glitterati	idolize	self-esteem	obsessed	airbrushed

We live in a world **1** .... with celebrity culture. It is impossible to move without hearing which star has fallen out with whom, what this **2** .... wisp of perfection was wearing on a trip to the shops yesterday and why this young identikit heart throb has decided to pen his autobiography at the **3** .... age of twenty five. But what effect is our obsession with the **4** .... having on our relationships? Why do we **5** .... them? What effect is our obsession with the toned, tanned and famous having on our body image and **6** ....?

Looking closely

1   What is the topic of this opinion piece?

2   Does the writer use facts or personal experience to make her point?

A couple of weeks ago a friend of mine hosted a jungle-themed party where everyone dressed up as the jungle animal of their choice. Banana cakes were served and my friend decorated her house (or rather, her parents' house) with trailing leaves and plastic spiders. Nothing so very unusual about that, you might say. Perhaps not, except that the age of the average guest was twenty-five, and there was not a child in sight. I watched, somewhat despairingly, as a roomful of overgrown monkeys and bush babies climbed over sofas and swung from the ceiling. Is it any wonder that my generation are known as 'the permanent adolescents'?

It's hard to imagine our parents' generation indulging in such pursuits. When my parents were twenty-five they had been working for seven years and had two small children. They lived in their own house, and had been financially independent since the day they started work. I believe their own leisure time was pretty limited: they would certainly not have spent it on throwing fancy dress parties.

Why would the 'Peter Pan' generation (as we are sometimes called) want to grow up though? After all, aren't we having fun? Don't we have the rest of our lives to get boring jobs and think serious thoughts? And didn't our poor parents live out boringly monochrome lives of hardship and self-denial? And yet, when I compare our pastimes, lifestyles and achievements with those of previous generations it is hard not to feel uneasy.

Language focus

1 Read the first paragraph of the opinion piece again. Tick three things the writer does.

a instantly conveys the writer's opinion on the subject ....

b asks a rhetorical question ....

c engages with the other side of the argument ....

d hints at a different topic which will be covered later ....

e refers to the writer's own personal experience ....

2 Read the first sentence of each paragraph. What function do these sentences perform?

Language note: topic sentences

Topic sentences come at the beginning of each paragraph and signpost the content of their paragraph. The rest of the paragraph then adds weight to the idea expressed in the topic sentence through examples, illustrations and evidence.

Useful tips

- Interesting opinion pieces voice strong opinions – this is one style of writing in which you do not have to consider the opposing side's point of view.
- Make your strongest point first – don't save it for your conclusion. Spend the rest of the piece backing it up with facts (researched or first hand).
- Use clear, powerful and direct language. Try to avoid hedging language like *seems* and *tends*.

Get writing

1 Choose one of these topics and write an opinion piece on it. Decide which angle you are going to approach it from. Think about how you can link your own experience to the topic, and what facts you can use to back up your opinion.

- Who does charity really help?
- It is best to wait until you are forty before having children.
- Teenagers do not leave home early enough.
- The rise of micro-blogging sites such as Twitter™ has killed our capacity for deep thinking.

Next steps

Keep a notebook of words which belong to the same lexical family. This will help you when you write opinion pieces. Next time you feel strongly about a contemporary issue, try writing an opinion piece. If you have a blog, post it there.

8 BEING CLEAR
Writing instructions for a friend

Getting started

1 In what different situations might you need to write instructions for a friend?
2 Think about a time when you had to read instructions from a friend. Were they easy to follow?

Looking closely

1 **Read the instructions and answer the questions.**

1 What are Katie's instructions for?
2 Are they easy to follow? Why?

Hi Stanya! Welcome to Barcelona! Hope you have a great stay. I'm sure you will... Help yourself to anything you need, okay? There are loads of figs on the tree outside in the garden – almost too many to eat! So thought you might like the recipe for my favourite cake!
Have fun!
Katie x

125g butter
125g yoghurt
250g caster sugar
2 eggs
310g self raising flour
12 figs (chopped up small)

1. Preheat the oven to 180C and grease the cake tin (you'll find it in the cupboard)

2. Mix the flour and sugar together.

3. Melt the butter, and add it to the mixture along with the figs, eggs and yoghurt.

4. Bake for one hour. The cake should be a nice golden brown colour.

5. Bon profit! As they say in Catalan...☺

Language focus

1 Which sentences are true for Katie's recipe? Which are true for her note? Write a tick in the correct place.

	Recipe	Note
1 The verbs come at the beginning of the sentence.	....	....
2 The sentences are long.	....	....
3 Katie uses adjectives.	....	....
4 Katie tells a joke.	....	....
5 The writing is simple.	....	....
6 Each step is on a different line and numbered.	....	....

2 Read these recipe extracts. Match the extract to the problem.

1 Pull the little thingy bits off the carrots.

a The recipe is written in the first person.

2 Add the butter and sift the flour while greasing the cake tin.

b The language here is vague and ambiguous.

3 I add the eggs one at a time.

c The writer has used an incorrect verb and the noun phrase is inaccurate.

4 Dredge the top with finely green cut of parsley.

d The writer's own opinion makes this instruction potentially confusing.

5 You might want to add some hot chillies, but personally I think it is much nicer without and you don't want to ruin the delicate flavour of the nettles, do you?

e This instruction includes three different and unrelated actions in the same step.

3 Rewrite the sentences in Exercise 2 so their meaning is clear.

4 Katie has left instructions on how to use her washing machine. Underline the language which is too vague. Rewrite her instructions to make them clearer.

Here's how you use the washing machine:
- Put some soap in the little drawer
- Twiddle the other button to select the temperature
- Push the button in
- The cycle takes ages and is very noisy – be warned

5 Katie has left instructions on how to defrost the fridge. Read the instructions and complete gaps 1–5 with sentences a–e. What effect does this have on the clarity of the instructions?

a It doesn't happen quickly – it takes a few hours.

b When you've taken all the stuff out, you'll see a little panel at the back of the fridge.

c You'll find that a lot of water drips onto the floor as the ice melts – that's normal.

d If you look behind the panel you'll see a lot of ice.

e You should find the fridge is a lot colder after this.

One more thing – you might find the fridge isn't working very well.
Sorry – I really need a new one! You can try defrosting it – this sometimes works.
Here's what to do ...
First, put some towels on the ground. **1**........ Then take all the food out of the fridge
and unplug it. **2**........ Unfasten the panel and pull it off. **3**........ You need to melt all this!
4........ You can try hitting the ice with a knife to speed things up. When the ice has
melted, put the panel back. Then plug the fridge in again. **5**........

Looking closely

1 Read these instructions from your friend and answer the questions.

1 Are they easy to follow?

2 What seems strange about the way in which they are written?

Hi,
Thanks very much for agreeing to look after the twins. I've written you some
instructions for bedtime so you know what to do.
6.45 p.m. Let the children watch TV while you run a bath. The bath water
needs to be about 32 degrees.
6.55 p.m. The children should be bathed. Supervise them at all times. They
should be given toys to play with. Make sure they aren't given anything which
will get ruined.
7.10 p.m. The children should be taken out of the bath before they begin to
squabble.
7.15 p.m. Dry them and put them to bed.
7.20 p.m. Read them a story.
Thanks, Chloe

Language focus

1 Which sentences do not use the present simple imperative? What do they use instead?

2 Is this suitable for instructions written for a friend? Where would you be more likely to find this kind of language?

Language note: sounding friendly

When writing instructions for a friend, it is important that your instructions are clear. However, you also want to sound friendly and not too formal. The best way to do this is to keep your instructions simple and short. Do not use the passive voice (*The children should be bathed*.) as this sounds very formal. You could also add one or two friendly remarks in brackets.

3 Read these friendly-sounding instructions and underline their formal equivalents in the note.

1 Chuck in some of their rubber ducks. That usually keeps them happy!

2 You'll not get off without a bedtime story …

3 Plonk them in front of the TV while you run the bath.

Useful tips

Keep your instructions as factual as possible. Avoid using *I* or *you* when writing instructions. Make sure your instructions follow a logical sequence, for example by using numbers or sequencing adverbs (*First, then, next*). If possible, ask someone to read your instructions. Would your reader be able to complete the task?

Get writing

1 Your friend has come for dinner and you have made your favourite dessert. She asks you if she can take the recipe home with her. Write out the recipe.

2 Your friend is house-sitting for you. Write instructions on how to use the cooker and washing machine.

Next steps

There are many opportunities to practise writing instructions in everyday life. Send an English-speaking friend a recipe you have written yourself. Make sure you find out how successfully your friend managed to follow your instructions.

9 BEING PRECISE AND FACTUAL
Writing a report

Getting started

1 Have you ever written a report about an important event?
2 What was the outcome of the report?
3 List the different situations in which you might have to write a concise and factual report about an event.

Looking closely

1 Read Laura's letter and answer the questions.

1 Why has she written it?
2 Do we know how Laura feels about the event?
3 What do you notice about the tone, language and content of this letter?

Dear Sir,

Policy number: XSG 1788

I am writing to make a claim on the above insurance policy to compensate for personal possessions which were damaged during my holiday in Puerto Pollensa, Majorca.

On the morning of Tuesday 15 October, the overflow pipe in the apartment where I was staying became disconnected from the storage tank. When I returned from the beach that afternoon, I found the apartment flooded and my personal possessions covered in water.

Fortunately, my clothes were not damaged in the deluge. However, my leather suitcase, which was brand new, has buckled under the pressure of the water. My laptop and camera were both severely water damaged and no longer work.

I have kept the damaged goods for your inspection and look forward to hearing from you.

Yours faithfully,

L. Conti.

Laura Conti

Language focus

1 Read Laura's letter again. Underline examples of the following:

1 precise language to describe what happened

2 factual and precise information about when the event happened

3 proof that the claim is genuine

4 factual and precise information about where the event happened

2 Read this extract from a travel insurance claim. Find three mistakes the writer makes.

> One day on my holiday I came back from a perfect day on the beach. I was so happy! Imagine how I felt when I saw that my apartment had burned to the ground. I sank to my knees, weeping, and rummaged in the ashes for remnants of my things but they were all gone. There had been a terrible fire caused by some electrical item in the apartment. Worst of all, my brand new camera was destroyed.

3 Rewrite the claim to make it more factual and objective.

4 Read this extract from a crime report. Rewrite it so that the details of the event are clear and the tone is factual.

> I was sitting at the bus station last week. I had a really heavy backpack with me and I'd been carrying it around with me for weeks so my back was getting really sore. I really needed to buy a drink and I couldn't face lugging it all the way over to the café so I asked this guy if he could watch it for me and he said okay. Anyway, I don't think I was all that long but when I came back the guy and my backpack had totally disappeared! My whole life was in that backpack – I'm totally gutted! Clothes, make-up, MP3 player – the lot.

5 Read these sentences from insurance claims. Why are they unclear?

1 The car lost control because it was going too fast.

2 I lost my wallet with all my money and lots of other really important stuff.

3 Finding it difficult to walk, we suspected the man was drunk.

4 On the last day of my holiday I broke my leg in a skiing accident.

6 Rewrite the sentences to make them clearer.

Language note: defining and non-defining relative clauses

Defining relative clauses add information. If they are removed, the meaning of the sentence changes. We do not use a comma to separate defining relative clauses.

The bedroom which is underneath the bathroom was badly water damaged. (The defining relative clause tells us which bedroom was damaged.)

Non-defining relative clauses give additional, non-essential information. If non-defining relative clauses are removed, the overall meaning of the sentence does not change. We use a comma to separate non-defining relative clauses.

My husband, who is a plumber, did all he could to stop the flood. (The non-defining relative clause provides extra information about the husband.)

7 **Read this sentence from Laura's report. What would change if Laura omitted the commas?**

However, my leather suitcase, which was brand new, has buckled under the pressure of the water.

8 **Read these sentences from insurance claims. Are the clauses defining relative clauses or non-defining relative clauses? In which sentences should commas be added?**

1 The fire which completely destroyed our house was caused by an electrical fault.

2 My daughter who was with me that day is still traumatised by the event.

3 The firefighters who arrived very quickly were unable to do anything.

4 My leg which was crushed by the falling bricks is still in plaster.

9 **Identify and correct the mistake made in each of the following sentences.**

1 My friend that came with me on holiday was also injured in the crash.

2 My passport which goes everywhere with me was in the small leather bag.

3 We stayed in the whitewashed hotel what has windows overlooking the sea.

4 My teacher who is also qualified in first aid she helped me stop my nosebleed.

5 The thief jumped into a white sports car who was wearing a leather jacket.

6 The hairdryer, which my husband had given me exploded while I was drying my hair.

Useful tips

- As you write your report, ask yourself not just *what?* but also *who, where, when, why, how?*
- Avoid emotive and subjective language. Keep your writing impartial and objective.
- Reports are not the place to speculate. Include only concrete facts.
- A report is a formal document. Do not use colloquialisms and abbreviations.
- Describe the event chronologically and be precise about dates and times.

10   Read the following car accident insurance claim. Rewrite it, so that the tone is appropriate, and correct any inaccurate use of relative clauses.

Dear Mr Peters,

On 15th December 2013 I was injured in an automobile accident with your insured, Angela Rogers. I was heading towards Lee River when I slowed down at some roadworks what were placed at the entrance of the bridge.

As I slowed down, your insured rammed into the back of my car. The force of the impact hurled me forwards and I felt a snapping sensation in my neck. Later that night I woke with a splitting headache who did not respond to painkillers. The pain gradually travelled down my neck and into my back. As a result of this injury, I was forced to miss out on many Christmas family gatherings over the festive period. My wife who is usually patient says I've been a misery to live with!

On top of the pain I have experienced, I have had to miss three weeks of building work, resulting in an estimated loss of earnings of £1,500. My back which still feels quite painful, is particularly sore when I am lifting heavy objects. This is hardly ideal for someone in my line of work.

As a result of this injury and my consequent considerable loss of earnings, I would like to be compensated £2,500.

I look forward to hearing from you at your earliest convenience.

Yours faithfully,
Kelvin Briggs

Get writing

1   You break your leg on the first day of your snowboarding holiday in Slovakia and have to spend two days in hospital before flying home earlier than planned. Write a report for your insurance company including all the details they will need to process your claim.

2   Your colleague gets badly injured at work when a photocopier falls off a table and onto her foot. She has to go to hospital immediately. As a witness, you are asked to write a report of the incident. Describe the incident. How did it happen? What action did you take?

Next steps

Have a look for websites devoted to funny insurance claims and read the claims there. See if you can identify why they are funny. What should the claimant have written instead?

10 IMPROVING Reviewing and editing your work

Getting started

1 What is the difference between reviewing your work and editing it?

2 What do you look for when you review your work? How do you go about editing it?

3 How often do you review your work?

Looking closely

1 Read the two texts. Who is the intended reader in each case?

2 Make a list of how you could improve each text.

Text A

From	SMartin@freemail.org
To	KGiles@officetoday.org
Subject:	Receptionist vacancy

Dear Mrs Giles,

I came across your ad for the post of receptionist online and am writing to attach my CV. I have worked in the customer service industry for ten years and have experience of working with an extremely long range of customers. I believe I have the stamina, attention to detail and enthusiasm which the position requires. One of my top hobbies is travel. I speak fluent French and German and this has always enabled me to get along very well with clients. Many thanks for your time in reading this email. I look forward to hearing from you.

Sam

Text B

Fieldstow today

| **Have your say** | News | Community | Schools | About |

Jakejoiner

Hi Keiko, I'm sorry but I don't agree with you at all. The building of a new store will be very beneficial to our town. So I am sorry to say I just don't agree with you! For a long time now, people have been forced to shop at overpriced small businesses where the customer service can sometimes leave a lot to be desire. This new store will bring a new breath of wind into our community. It will also heighten employment, and I think will give people new pride in their town. Why would we want to live in the past anyway? For many years now people have been complaining that they don't have where to shop for cheap and fashion items. Now they can find what they want.

Language note: reviewing and editing

When you review your work, you check that it says what you wanted it to say. You should assess the content and structure of your work, and focus on paragraphs and how well you have developed your argument.

Editing is more about fine-tuning your work. You should look at sentence structure, grammar errors, spelling, punctuation and word choice.

It is important to approach this part of the writing process very seriously. Find a quiet place where you will not be disturbed.

Language focus

1   Which of the following should you assess at the reviewing stage? Write a tick where appropriate.

1	tense agreement	....	**6**	spelling	....
2	collocations	....	**7**	punctuation	....
3	structure	....	**8**	word choice	....
4	paragraphing	....	**9**	links between ideas	....
5	sentence structure	....	**10**	content	....

2   Read the texts again. What would you change at the reviewing stage?

3   Rewrite the texts, dividing them into paragraphs where necessary.

4   Is there anything you would add to the content of Text A? What might you omit from Text B?

5   Look at Text A again. What do you notice about the sentence structure? What changes could you make to improve this?

6   Katrin is applying for a new job and her English teacher has written her a reference. Read and review this first draft reference, using the ideas in Exercises 1–5 to help you.

   1   What problems might there be with the draft?

   2   Rewrite the draft to solve these problems.

Katrin is a friendly, conscientious and hard-working student. She has always impressed me with her punctuality, creativity and positive attitude. Katrin has just split up with her boyfriend, and I am sure a change of scene would be really beneficial for her too. I have been Katrin's English teacher for five years, and she has performed consistently well in classroom assignments. She actually works very well with groups and individually. Last year she deservedly won our Student of the Year award. I cannot recommend Katrin's work highly enough: she would be an asset to any organisation.

Looking closely

1 Read the five texts and identify the purpose of each one.

A ....

B ....

C ....

D ....

E ....

Text A

> Vlad is highly motivaited and organized. His dynamic, enthusiastic naiture has made him very popular in our deportment. Vlad can always be rallied upon to produce his best work and has a wonderful eye for detayle. I will be very sorry to lose him, but I am sure that his unflaging energy will be of great servise to him and others in the work he is hopping to do.

Text B

> I am writing with regards to the high levels of noise in my neighbourhood between the hours of ten o'clock in the evening and two o'clock in the morning – I am aware that us city dwellers cannot expect complete tranquillity – however I genuinely believe, that the constant levels of noise and disturbance in the street outside our house are having a negative impact on my family's health!!

Text C

> You had asked me about the location of our flat. We are living in the Saint Denis area of Paris, within easy walking distance of some wonderful shops and cafes. There is a tram stop just beside our house, so you could travel around the city very easy. I see from your Flat Swap profile that you are interested in history – will you be planning to visit some our world famous museums?

Text D

> Please accept my deepest gratitude for writing this most enlightening post. My sentiments were deeply aroused my your insights into the trials of learning English grammar.

Text E

> In this age of tall unemployment and strong financial hardship it is understandable that such a wide amount of people choose to search their fortune abroad.

Language note: a two-part process

Texts A–E above are all examples of texts which may have been successfully *reviewed* but which have not been *edited* – they are well structured but they still have lots of little mistakes throughout them. It is extremely important to make sure that you include both reviewing *and* editing in your writing process. One is not worthwhile without the other.

Language focus

1 Match texts A–E to the most obvious type of error 1–5.

1 punctuation ....
2 tense errors ....
3 spelling ....

4 word choice (collocations) ....
5 register ....

2 Rewrite the five texts, focusing on the errors you identified in Exercise 1. Use *Appendix 4: Proofreading* to help you.

Useful tips

- Read your work for comprehension first. After all, the important thing is that you have managed to get your point across. You can focus on other mistakes later.
- Read what you have written from your intended reader's point of view. Have you used the appropriate level of formality throughout?
- Use a collocations dictionary to check that your word choice is correct. You can find a range of dictionaries at **www.collinsdictionary.com**.
- Read your writing aloud. This is the best way to check that what you have written reads well. If you stumble over something you have written, it means you need to rewrite it.

Get writing

1 Review and edit three of the writing tasks you have completed in this book. Choose tasks from three different writing genres.

Next steps

Write your own checklist, placing particular emphasis on the mistakes you know you are most guilty of making, whether this be a difficulty with a particular grammatical tense or a problem with punctuation.

After you have reviewed and edited your work, consider what you feel are your particular strengths and weaknesses as a writer. If possible, ask a friend or a teacher for their opinion too. This will help you to focus on improving your writing. As well as reviewing and editing your own work, volunteer to edit the work of your friends and peers.

11 SHOWING DISAPPOINTMENT
Writing a letter of complaint

Getting started

1 Have you ever made a complaint in writing?
2 Was your complaint dealt with in a satisfactory way?
3 What are the benefits of making a written complaint as opposed to making a telephone call?

Looking closely

1 Read the email. What two aspects of his trip does Jovan complain about?

2 Do you think Jovan's email is likely to achieve the result he would like? Explain why or why not.

From: jovangagic56@memail.com
To: kmallory@LN.org
Subject: Hi!

Dear Mr Mallory,

I am writing to express my deep disappointment with regard to my experience at Lingua Nova English summer school in the first two weeks of July. I had been thoroughly looking forward to learning English and learning about culture in the UK, but I am afraid that my time at your summer school failed to live up to my expectations.

Your brochure clearly states that the student accommodation is situated "in the heart of Edinburgh". This is misleading as my accommodation was, in fact, situated a good fifty minutes bus ride from the city centre in what I can only describe as a less than picturesque part of the suburbs.

Furthermore, the activity programme did not reflect the fact that we were located in one of Europe's most interesting and historical cities: one evening activity consisted of a walk to a nearby retail park, another was a trip to a bowling alley. Finally, on our one trip into the city centre our "guide" readily admitted that she was not from Edinburgh, and had in fact never visited the city before. I had been eagerly anticipating a guided tour of Scotland's treasures. In fact, I was dumped in the city centre with no map and told to "check things out" while your employee went shopping in Princes Street.

This was a long awaited, once in a lifetime trip and cost me over two years' hard work and saving. Although I do have positive memories of my trip (my English teachers were dedicated, knowledgeable and inspiring), the accommodation and activities programme were wholly unsatisfactory.

I would like to be refunded for my accommodation and would really appreciate a reply within the next two weeks.

Yours sincerely,

Jovan Gagic

Language note: tone

The tone of a piece of writing expresses your attitude to what you are writing about, and could, for example, be angry, humorous, disappointed or sarcastic. Purpose and tone are very closely related. If you are clear about why you are writing something, this will help you decide on the appropriate tone. The words and expressions you choose help you create the tone you desire.

Language focus

1. Which word best describes the overall tone of Jovan's email?

sarcastic	angry	wistful	hostile
threatening	disappointed	humorous	apologetic

2. Underline the words and expressions which helped you to choose your answer.

3. The writer puts phrases in inverted commas (") three times in his email. What effect does this have in each case?

4. What effect does Jovan want his email to have on Mr Mallory? Tick the answers which apply.
   - ☐ to make him feel angry
   - ☐ to make him feel worried
   - ☐ to make him feel ashamed of himself
   - ☐ to make him feel sorry for Jovan
   - ☐ to make him laugh
   - ☐ to make him rethink his staff recruitment and training procedures

Language note: remaining tactful

It is important to remain tactful and polite when you are writing a complaint. Instead of using a negative adjective (*disgusting, appalling, horrendous*), Jovan uses the adjective *picturesque* and then negates it by saying *less than*. This makes his complaint more polite and simultaneously, emphasizes his point.

Looking closely

1. Read this extract from a letter of complaint. What is the tone of this extract? What effect might it have on the reader?

Firstly, the breakfasts. Now, I know that you Scots don't exactly have a reputation for great cooking, but a grown man requires more than half a bowl of grey gloop in the morning. I never did quite work out what the lumps of lukewarm black gristle under the hotplate were – maybe if I had felt brave enough to try, I would have had the energy to take part in all of these wonderfully exciting and informative cultural tours you'd laid on for us (not!).

2. Underline the offensive parts of the extract.

Language focus

1   Read these sentences from Jovan's email. What effect does the underlined word or phrase have? Replace the underlined words with the words in brackets. Does this emphasize or weaken his point?

1   I am <u>afraid</u> that my time at your summer school failed to live up to my expectations. (sorry)

2   Finally, on our one trip into the city centre our "guide" <u>readily</u> admitted that she was not from Edinburgh, and had in fact never visited the city before. (grudgingly)

3   I was <u>dumped</u> in the city centre with no map … (dropped off)

4   This was a long awaited, once in a lifetime trip for me and cost me <u>over two years' hard work and saving</u>. (just over £3000 in total)

5   I <u>would like to be</u> refunded for my accommodation … (insist on being)

2   Lara has just returned from an unsatisfactory meal in a restaurant. Underline the most appropriate word or phrase.

To	sslater@corleonisrestaurant.com
From:	llcellini1985@usbcthub.co.au
Subject:	Dinner this evening

Dear Mrs Slater,

I have just returned from a/an **1** *very disappointing / unpleasant* meal at your restaurant.
As you know, I am a regular customer and have always been **2** *delighted / quite happy* with the quality of the service and the food.

However, the meal I ate tonight **3** *fell far short of my expectations / was bordering on inedible.*
Our steaks were **4** *virtually raw / seriously undercooked* and the accompanying potatoes were cold. While your waiter was clearly **5** *unable to cope with the volume of customers / experiencing a busy night* I felt that he was **6** *rude and abrupt / somewhat distracted* when I voiced my disappointment.

To make matters worse, the meal was a treat for my aunt's 70th birthday. What should have been an enjoyable experience turned into a **7** *culinary nightmare / less than relaxing evening.*

I would like to express my disappointment at this evening's events. I would also
8 *appreciate your reassurance / demand a guarantee* that this will not happen again.

Yours sincerely,

Lara Cellini

Useful tips

- Before you start writing, gather all the facts you need to help you make your complaint, e.g. relevant dates, times, names and quotations.
- Keep your complaint concise and to the point. Focus on what it is that you find unsatisfactory and avoid going off on tangents.
- Be explicit about the action you want your reader to take, and give a date by which you would like your complaint dealt with.
- It is important, where possible, to mention any positive experiences you have had with the company. If your reader views you as a potentially valuable future client they are more likely to wish to help you.
- Remember that your reader is a human being too. Avoid making threats and saying hurtful things.
- Refer to *Appendix 1: Useful phrases* for some good handy phrases and to ensure that you are using the correct level of formality when you write.

Get writing

1 **Rewrite this extract from a letter of complaint. Use a disappointed tone similar to the one in Jovan's email on page 48.**

> I stupidly wore these shoes to an interview. On my way out of the interview room the heel snapped off totally and I was made to look a complete and utter fool in front of the entire panel. Hardly surprising I didn't get the job is it – who would employ someone with such lousy taste in shoes? So thanks to you and your rotten shoe company, I've lost out on my dream job and possibly any chance of future success in my chosen career.

2 **Write a letter of complaint for these situations. Use an appropriate tone.**

1 You have just returned from a summer holiday in the Pyrénées. You had booked a family apartment in a quiet mountain retreat and had been looking forward to the lovely tranquil garden mentioned in the brochure. However, the house was excessively noisy due to building work being carried out next door. Furthermore, the garden was dusty and littered with rubbish from the building site. You want compensation.

2 You have been going to your local restaurant for many years and know the owners quite well. Recently the restaurant has employed some new waiting staff who are impolite and unfriendly. Last night, you were pointedly ignored for half an hour before one of them took your order. You would like an explanation.

Next steps

Become aware of tone when you are reading. If you notice that a piece of writing has a particular tone, underline the words and expressions which tell you what the writer's tone is.

You can find many examples of complaint emails online. Read some of these and decide whether or not they are effective. Think about how you could rewrite the ineffective complaint emails.

12 BEING POLITE BUT FIRM
Writing a delicate email

Getting started

1 When did you last have to write a delicate email? What was the situation?

2 Did you find it difficult to write? What response did your email receive?

Looking closely

1 **Read the email and answer the questions.**

1 What is the relationship between Klara and Malu?

2 What does Klara ask Malu to do?

2 **How do you think Malu will respond to Klara's email? Why do you think this?**

To	malu90@freemail.org
Subject:	Hi!

Dear Malu,

Hope you're well and enjoying this fine summer weather. Plenty of good opportunities for surfing where you are, I should think!

I was in the cottage at Gnadenwald last weekend and spotted a couple of things I thought I might ask you about. Have there been a few casualties in the crockery department? I had difficulty finding a breakfast bowl for my cornflakes, although I distinctly remember buying a set of six bowls at the beginning of May. I was also wondering if you might be able to shed some light on what has happened to the white living room rug – I was a bit surprised to find it has been totally ruined – are these coffee stains?

Being a bit of a butterfingers myself, I know only too well that these things happen. Heinz doesn't call me Calamity Klara for nothing! Having said that, it would be great if you could let me know when accidents happen and replace or repair broken items. I am more than happy to let my friends have free use of the cottage, but I really do like everything to be shipshape for my own visits. Spending the first day of a long weekend emptying bins and hoovering isn't exactly my idea of a good time!

It was great to hear about your new job by the way. I knew that red jacket would go down well at interview!

Take care and speak soon,

Klara

Language focus

1 Underline examples of the following in Klara's email.

1 an indirect question
2 a friendly, conversational opening comment
3 a self-deprecating remark
4 a request for action
5 a polite and friendly closing remark
6 a euphemism

2 What effect do these examples have on the email?

3 Underline the two examples of the passive voice in Klara's email.

4 Choose one example from Exercise 3. Rewrite this sentence using the active voice. What do you notice?

5 Match the sentences in the active voice to their passive equivalents. Which sound less combative?

1 You totally ruined my new shoes.
2 You haven't washed up.
3 You spilled coffee on my new rug.
4 You stole my pen.

a I see the dishes haven't been washed.
b My new rug has been badly stained.
c My pen has been stolen.
d My new shoes have been ruined.

Looking closely

1 Read the email. What is the relationship between Alex and Ms Tallis?

Dear Ms Tallis,

I'm just writing to check whether you've received my invoice for the series of training workshops I led in May. The amount has not yet been transferred into my account, although I completed the work three months ago. As I'm sure you are aware, I run a small-scale business from home and work to a tight budget, so it is therefore very important that I get paid on time.

Please could you check with the accounts department that the invoice has been processed and let me know when I can expect payment for my work?

With many thanks and best regards,

Alex Loman

Language focus

1 What features does this email share with Klara's email? How does it differ?

2 Does Alex use humour in this email? Why / Why not?

3 Read Alex's email again. Underline examples of sentences with a human subject. Then underline examples of sentences with impersonal subjects. What effect does choice of subject have on the overall tone of the email?

4 Rewrite the sentences so that they sound more delicate and less negative. It may help you to refer to *Appendix 1: Useful phrases* for guidance.

1 You haven't paid me yet.

....

2 You haven't been returning my phone calls.

....

3 I will not tolerate this situation.

....

4 If you can't afford to pay me, I will be forced to take further action.

....

5 You have insulted me and the pride I take in my work.

....

Get writing

1 Read the email from Andris to Tadas. Do you think that Andris will get what he wants? Rewrite his email to make it more direct.

Hey Tadas,

How are things with you? Fernando tells me you're going to his birthday weekend in Berlin – looks like it'll be a fun weekend!
I dunno if I'll make it. I've been feeling pretty broke recently and should probably think about saving up for starting my course next year. Don't suppose there's any chance of getting that hundred quid back from you, is there? No worries if not …

Have fun in Berlin!

Andris

2   Rewrite the email to make it more polite.

Dear Rosita,

You haven't attended English class for six weeks now. This means that I have no choice but to issue you with a warning. If you do not resume attending classes within one week, I will withhold your class certificate and you will lose your place on the course.

Please note that you have failed to submit your last three essays too.

Regards,

Dinara Antonovich

3   You work in a busy office. Recently one of your colleagues has resigned, and your workload has become increasingly heavy. You are working overtime every night, without receiving any extra pay or recognition. Write a polite but firm email to your line manager explaining the situation and asking for action to be taken.

4   In your free time you run an outdoor club for teenagers. The club has been a great success. However, recently a new recruit has started bullying the other members. You would like the boy's parents to know about their son's behaviour and talk to him about it.

Next steps

Look through your email inbox and sent folder. How many examples can you find of delicate emails? Read them carefully, and decide how effective they are.

13 REMAINING BALANCED
Writing about a cause you believe in

Getting started

1 What causes do you feel strongly about? Why?
2 Have you ever written a letter on behalf of a cause you support? If so, what was the outcome?
3 How effective do you think these kinds of letters are?

Looking closely

1 Read the two letters and answer the questions.

1 What are they about?
2 What action do they request?
3 Who is Mr Howard?

2 Which letter is more likely to make a difference and why?

Text A

15th January 2014

Dear Mr Howard,

I was absolutely shocked and horrified to discover your company uses pulp and paper sourced from endangered rainforests in the manufacture of your children's toys. When I saw the footage of poor homeless tigers on the television I was moved to tears of deep sorrow. As a social worker and charity volunteer, I would rather die than give my children toys made by Play Time.

You, and all the other fat cats like you, luxuriate in your plundered millions while innocent creatures endure misery and uncertain futures. You make me sick.

I have told all my friends about the crimes you have committed. You must find another source for your materials; a source which does not harm any more precious forests. Please let me know your intentions on this matter.

Yours sincerely,

F. Cosenza

Francesco Cosenza

Text B

Dear Mr Howard,

It has recently come to my attention that Play Time's toys are manufactured using pulp and paper sourced from endangered rainforests. The plight of these rainforest's endangered wildlife has been publicized recently in the international press and world media. As a primary school teacher and mother of two young children, I do not want to buy toys which are manufactured with so little regard for the earth's finite resources.

Furthermore, it is well known that you make great profits from the sale of your toys, while doing nothing at all to offset the environmental damage your actions result in. This is unacceptable.

It is time for you to confront the serious consequences your industry is having on the environment, and find a more sustainable source for your products. Please tell me what you plan to do to address this urgent matter.

Yours sincerely,

Rana Balbay

Rana Balbay

Language focus

1 **Look at these phrases from Text A. Underline the equivalent phrases in Text B.**

   1 I was absolutely shocked and horrified to discover your company uses pulp and paper sourced from endangered rainforests in the manufacture of your children's toys.

   2 When I saw the footage of poor homeless tigers on the television I was moved to tears of deep sorrow.

   3 You, and all the other fat cats like you, luxuriate in your plundered millions while innocent creatures endure misery and uncertain futures.

   4 You make me sick.

   5 You must find another source for your materials; a source which does not harm any more precious forests.

2 **Underline language in Exercise 1 which is subjective or biased.**

Language note: remaining balanced

When writing letters about a cause you believe in, it is important to distance yourself from your own feelings, however strong they may be, and to come across as someone who has carefully considered the facts. Aim for an objective tone in your writing, rather than a subjective one. This means writing in a factual, balanced and non-emotional way. *This is unacceptable* not *You make me sick.*

3 Match the objective words to the subjective words with a similar meaning.

1	work	**a**	tyrant
2	crowd	**b**	appalling
3	suffer	**c**	mob
4	unsatisfactory	**d**	toil
5	boss	**e**	experience

4 Which sentences are subjective? Which are neutral?

1 Defenceless animals are being slaughtered by these barbaric practices.

2 It is absolutely devastating that these magnificent forests are being cut down.

3 This country is not equipped to deal with a major oil spill.

4 Many of the workers at these factories are young women from rural areas.

5 For too long, unscrupulous bosses have been pocketing the profits.

Looking closely

1 Read Claudia's email and underline the most appropriate word or phrase.

Dear Mr Towell,

It has come to my attention that your cosmetics company uses products which are tested on **1** *animals / defenceless little rabbits* I was **2** *absolutely flabbergasted / very concerned* to read about this in the national press and would like you to know that I find this practice **3** *unacceptable / despicable.*

Many other leading cosmetic companies now test their beauty products dermatologically as this is recognized to be **4** *humane and ethical practice / far and away the kindest thing to do.*

Please confirm that you have taken steps to **5** *address this very important matter / free these vulnerable creatures* I look forward to hearing from you.

Yours sincerely,

Claudia Marwick

Language focus

1 Underline the parts of Claudia's letter which tell us:

1 the issue she is writing about.

2 how she feels about this issue.

3 supporting evidence she provides to back up her request.

4 the action she wants taken.

2 Rewrite the sentences to make them sound neutral and objective. It may help you to refer to *Appendix 1: Useful phrases* for guidance.

1 The new motorway will make hundreds of poor woodland creatures homeless.

2 You must stop this cruel practice of testing make-up on poor little bunnies and mice.

3 Global warming is slowly baking life on this planet – it is a terrible shame for humanity.

4 Hundreds of gifted and hardworking children will lose their chance of a better future if you close down their school.

Useful tips

- Keep your letter factual and polite. Avoid sounding aggressive.
- Be positive. Assume that your reader is open to reasoned argument and that your request stands a good chance of being granted.
- Write a little about who you are, so your reader knows where you are coming from.
- Show that you expect a reply. Use one of the useful phrases from Appendix 1 in your concluding paragraph.

Get writing

1 Plans are underway for a large superstore to be built in your town. You are concerned about the impact that this will have on your local small businesses. Write a letter to your local council planning department, outlining your objections and requesting a public vote on the matter.

2 You have recently read a report on the unsatisfactory conditions experienced by workers on banana plantations. Write a letter to your local convenience store, asking them to confirm that they buy their bananas from suppliers who pay their workers a fair wage.

3 It has come to your attention that a leading toy manufacturer is using chemical compounds in the toys they produce. Studies have linked these chemicals to a range of different cancers. Write a letter stating your concern and requesting action.

Next steps

Many campaign organizations encourage people to write letters on their behalf and provide guidance on letter writing. Find the website of an organization campaigning for a cause you believe in. Read the sample letters and note down any useful phrases and expressions. Write a letter on behalf of the organization.

14 BEING LIGHT-HEARTED
Writing a personal anecdote

Getting started

1 Why might you write a personal anecdote?

2 How would you make it enjoyable to read?

3 Think about something you have read recently which made you smile. How did the writer achieve this effect?

Looking closely

1   Julia is working in Hungary for a year and has included this anecdote on her blog. Read the blog post and answer the questions.

1 What is the purpose of this anecdote?

2 Why do you think Julia didn't invite Brett on her walk? What mistake does she make?

3 Why was her neighbour confused?

My year on the Puszta

| Home | My news | Gallery | Contact |

A selfish spring stroll

Posted on 15 March

Spring has sprung here after an endless and freezing winter. I'd been slaving over a hot photocopier all day and couldn't wait to get out and enjoy a refreshing walk by the river Tisza, breathing in the balmy air and listening to the chirrup of the birds. So I sprinted up to the flat, dumped my briefcase in the hall, called a quick 'hello' to Brett and then dashed out again, locking the door behind me.

Yes, I locked the door, leaving Brett unable to get out of the stifling hot flat! While I wandered barefoot and carefree on the grassy riverbanks, Brett was completely unable to appreciate the first night of spring. Have I mentioned that there is only one window in our flat and that it is jammed? (We've been meaning to get it fixed for ages ...)

Well, Brett was determined to free himself at any cost, and in desperation he knelt down in front of the door, peered through the letter box and decided to call for help to the next person he saw. This next person happened to be the elderly man who lives above us. Poor Brett mustered up all the Hungarian he knew and called out 'Can you help me?' (It turned out later that he had actually been calling 'I can help you!') Our poor neighbour looked around him, clearly shaken that a letter box was offering him assistance and beat a hasty retreat back upstairs.

When I returned from my blissful spring stroll I felt terrible to find that Brett had spent the entire evening kneeling in front of the letter box. Needless to say we have both made resolutions. I will stop and think before I rush off on any more impulsive strolls, and Brett is learning Hungarian grammar!

Language focus

1 Number the events of the anecdote in the correct order.

  a Brett decided to learn Hungarian grammar. ....

  b Spring arrived after a long, cold winter. ....

  c Brett asked a neighbour for help. ....

  d Julia was desperate to go out and enjoy the fine weather. ....

  e Julia felt terrible when she realized that Brett had been locked in. ....

  f Julia accidentally locked Brett in the flat. ....

2 Underline the verbs in the anecdote. What different tenses has the writer used?

....

....

....

Language note: past perfect and past perfect continuous

When we are telling a story in the past simple tense, we can use the past perfect simple and past perfect continuous to refer to things which happened before the narrative began. We can also use the past perfect to show that someone is reflecting on something which happened prior to the events of the story.

*I **had been rushing** around at work all day, and was totally exhausted.*

*That's when I **realized** that **I'd left** my wallet in the supermarket!*

*I often thought about how easy my life **had been** back then.*

---

3 Underline the correct tense in each sentence.

  1 I was exhausted and absolutely starving – I had *travelled / been travelling* for ages.

  2 We *had been wandering / wandered* around for what seemed like hours, when we finally found the hotel.

  3 We caught the bus just as it *was pulling out / pulled out* of the station.

  4 The first time I saw Venice, I immediately *fell / had fallen* in love with it.

  5 I was almost at the airport when I realized I'd *left / been leaving* my passport at home!

4 Rewrite these short anecdotes using the past perfect (you will need to begin with the last action).

  1 Francisco lost his job. He failed his exams. He decided to look for work in another country.

  2 Marie and Daniel had a long and tiring journey. On their journey they were robbed. They arrived at their hotel at midnight.

  3 Ludovic spent the whole day cooking. He baked an enormous rhubarb cake. His guest arrived for dinner and said she was on a diet.

  4 Mark won a lot of money in a competition. He bought a camper van. He went travelling around the world.

5   Read Julia's anecdote on page 60 again. What makes it light-hearted in tone? Underline the words or phrases which help you choose your answer.

6   Match the words from the anecdote to their meanings.

1	slave	**a**	suffocating, causing difficulties in breathing
2	stifling	**b**	look with difficulty or concentration at something
3	peer	**c**	work excessively hard
4	blissful	**d**	walk in a leisurely way
5	stroll	**e**	extremely happy, joyful

7   What effect does each word in Exercise 6 have on Julia's anecdote?

8   Read the short anecdote and underline the most appropriate word to make it interesting and light-hearted in tone.

We finally arrived in Prague, cold and hungry. There had been no buffet carriage on the train and we had **1** *eaten / scoffed* the last of our sandwiches the day before. I was **2** *dreaming / thinking* of hot soup and dumplings followed by a sound night's sleep in a warm and cosy bed.

Our guidebook had assured us that every train arriving in Prague was met by a **3** *gaggle / group* of mother **4** *types / hens* offering accommodation in their nearby guesthouses. But no such motherly souls met us on the **5** *empty / deserted* platform. Instead, a tall **6** *thin / gaunt* man in a long black coat **7** *walked / shuffled* towards us. He pulled a scrap of paper from his pocket and showed us a photo of a dark and bare room. As I realized that this might just be our host for the evening I began to feel even colder than I had before.

Useful tips

- A good personal anecdote has a strong beginning, middle and an ending. Plan what you want to say before you start writing.
- While planning your anecdote, make a list of all the questions your reader might want to ask, e.g. *Where were you? Who were you with? How were you feeling?* Answer these questions in your writing.
- Use a range of narrative tenses. Remember you can use the past perfect tense to set your scene.
- Keep the tone chatty and conversational. Read your work aloud – how do the words you have chosen sound?
- Readers are more likely to be entertained by a humorous account of something which has gone wrong. (An account of a perfect day is unlikely to entertain).
- Remember that humour is best directed at yourself – not at other people. For example, *How could I have been so stupid?* is more effective than *How could she have been so stupid?*

Looking closely

1 Reorder the paragraphs in this anecdote so that there is a clear beginning, middle and an end.

> **1** Unfortunately, my weekend in Paris was memorable for all the wrong reasons. Our hotel was in urgent need of a facelift – the rooms were damp and dirty and we could hardly sleep as our beds were so uncomfortable.
>
> **2** As if that wasn't bad enough, my friend got food poisoning on our first night there and spent the whole weekend in bed. I arrived at the airport feeling quite relieved to be homeward bound – only to find when we got to the check in desk that I'd left my passport at the hotel. What a disaster!
>
> **3** I had never been to Paris before, so you can imagine my delight when my best friend said she had won two tickets for a weekend break there – and she had chosen me to accompany her!

2 Is there any information the writer has not included which you think might improve this anecdote?

Get writing

1 Think about an interesting experience you once had on your travels. Write an anecdote about it. Make sure you include all the information your reader needs to know.

2 Choose one of the feelings in the box, and think of a time you felt this way. Write a light-hearted anecdote describing the situation.

embarrassed	terrified	in despair	bored	exhausted

3 Pick an event you remember from your childhood. Write a humorous anecdote describing it. Focus on your feelings and make your account as descriptive as you can.

Next steps

Write down a personal anecdote you enjoy telling people.

Start keeping a written record of amusing anecdotes you hear. Next time you hear one you enjoy, write it down, bearing in mind what you have learned in this unit.

15 CREATING MOOD
Writing a short story

Getting started

1 Do you often read fiction? What do you like to read?
2 Have you ever written a story in English?
3 What are the ingredients of a good short story?

Looking closely

1 Read the beginning of Ray Bradbury's short story *The Illustrated Man* and answer the questions.

1 How many characters are in this extract?
2 Why do you think the Illustrated Man does not unbutton his shirt?
3 What do you think will happen next?

It was a warm afternoon in early September when I first met the Illustrated Man. Walking along an asphalt road, I was on the final leg of a two weeks' walking tour of Wisconsin. Late in the afternoon I stopped, ate some pork, beans and a doughnut, and was preparing to stretch out and read when the Illustrated Man walked over the hill and stood for a moment against the sky.

I didn't know he was Illustrated then. I only knew that he was tall, once well muscled, but now, for some reason, going to fat. I recall that his arms were long, and the hands thick, but that his face was like a child's, set upon a massive body.

He seemed only to sense my presence, for he didn't look directly at me when he spoke his first words:

'Do you know where I can find a job?'
'I'm afraid not,' I said.
'I haven't had a job that's lasted in forty years,' he said.
Though it was a hot late afternoon, he wore his wool shirt buttoned tight about his neck. His sleeves were rolled and buttoned down over his thick wrists. Perspiration was streaming from his face, yet he made no move to open his shirt.
'Well,' he said at last, 'this is as good a place as any to spend the night. Do you mind company?'
'I have some extra food you'd be welcome to,' I said.
He sat down heavily, grunting. 'You'll be sorry you asked me to stay,' he said. 'Everyone always is.'

Language focus

1 Choose the word which best describes the mood of the story.

upbeat   nostalgic

humorous   reflective

ominous

2 Underline the words and phrases which helped you to choose your answer.

> **Language note: mood**
>
> *Mood* describes how the reader feels when reading. Through skilful use of language (word choice, dialogue, description, etc.) you can create whatever mood you need to when you are writing creatively.

3 Identify the mood in these texts. Underline the words which helped you to choose your answer.

Text A

> The woman who sold me my newspaper looked remarkably like a large, contented tabby cat – so much so that I could have sworn I heard her purr as I left the shop.

Text B

> When a man grows up in the shadow of his infinitely better looking and more popular brother he learns to cultivate his mind and always to be smarter than they expect.

Text C

> It was a desolate place. I closed my eyes and listened to the fierce squall of the gulls and the roar of the sea thundering against the rocks below.

4 Read Text C again. Think of a contrasting mood and rewrite the extract to reflect the mood you have chosen.

5 Read the beginning of this scary story. Choose the correct words to create a sinister mood.

> Darkness had slowly managed to trick its way into the **1** *bare / cosy* room where the old woman sat, her **2** *gnarled / dimpled* fingers stroking a **3** *fluffy / skinny* grey cat. Outside the wind **4** *blew / howled* and shook the trees. Bare branches **5** *thumped / tapped* on the glass and seemed to beckon her outside.

6 Look at the extract from *The Illustrated Man* again. Do you think this is a good beginning for a short story? Explain why or why not.

Language note: characters

When writing a short story you do not have the time to describe your characters in as detailed a way as you would if you were writing a novel. Your characters' defining qualities must be revealed in as few words as possible – by a mannerism, a facial expression or a particular item of clothing.

He was a thin, angry-looking man with skin which looked as if he had just brushed up against a cheese grater.

She pushed past me impatiently, all jagged elbows and astringent perfume.

The shop assistant was a plump, grinning cat of a woman. She gently waggled her chins in greeting.

7 Close your eyes and imagine 'the illustrated man'. What do you see? Look at the text again and underline the words which have given you this impression.

8 Read this summary of the rest of *The Illustrated Man*. Number the events in the correct order.

a The narrator runs away from the Illustrated Man. ....

b The narrator meets the Illustrated Man one hot afternoon in the countryside. ....

c The Illustrated Man falls asleep. The narrator sees that one of the tattoos shows the Illustrated Man murdering him. ....

d The Illustrated Man reveals his tattoos: the figures in his tattoos are alive and tell stories of the future. ....

9 Match the elements of a plot to their definitions.

1	Beginning	**a**	Introduce a problem or conflict. One of your characters should have an obstacle to overcome.
2	Rising action	**b**	Introduce your setting and characters.
3	Climax	**c**	Show the results of your characters' actions and wind up the story.
4	Resolution	**d**	This is the main event of your story. Your character should face their obstacle.

10 Reread the summary of *The Illustrated Man* in Exercise 8. Match the events of the story to the elements of the plot.

Useful tips

- As usual, think of your audience. Even better, *think* of *one* person you are writing this story for, e.g. your best friend, your mother, your son. If you write for too general an audience your writing will not be strong and focused enough.
- Write clearly, yet descriptively. You can create memorable pictures in just a few words.
- Involve your readers' five senses. Think not only of how things look, but also how they feel, smell, sound and taste.
- Choose your words carefully in order to create the mood you have chosen.
- Decide who is telling the story. Are you going to use first person narration (*I*) or third person (*He / She*)?

Get writing

1 Close your eyes and picture someone (it can be someone you know well or someone you have never met). Write a paragraph describing this person's appearance, focusing on the things which make them unique and interesting.

2 Think of the person you described in Exercise 1 and place them in a location (a desert island, a crowded city, a meadow). What are they doing? Write the beginning of a story in which you set the scene and establish your character. Choose the most important elements of the description you wrote in Exercise 1 to give the reader a picture of your character.

3 Read what you have written. Have you created a strong mood? Choose one of the moods below and rewrite the beginning of your story. Convey the mood to your reader through word choice, character description and dialogue.

joyful	creepy	wistful
resigned	humorous	

4 Continue your story. Introduce conflict, create a climax and finish with a resolution.

Next steps

Visit a creative writing website where writers post their stories, and read and comment constructively on the work of others. Giving and receiving feedback in this way focuses you on your strengths and areas for development.

Read some short stories in English and decide which ones you like best. Incorporate elements of your favourite writers' style into your own work. Have a look at the Collins English Readers at **www.collinselt.com/readers**.

16 COMMUNICATING EMOTION
Writing a speech

Getting started

1 Have you ever made a speech? What was the occasion?
2 In what different situations might you be required to write and deliver a speech?
3 What is the best speech you have listened to?

Looking closely

1 **Read the speech below, and answer the questions.**

1 Why has the speech been written?
2 What emotions are being portrayed through the speaker's choice of words and phrasing?
3 Do you think the speech is effective? Why?

When I look around this room, I see faces alive with vitality and energy. I can only conclude that you must have all stopped for an energizing, quality coffee at one of this town's wonderful, independent coffee shops on the way here. But seriously, I would like to thank each and every one of you for coming here tonight.

I know we are all here for the same reason. We are here because not one of us is willing to lose the town we love. In a recent survey carried out by the town council, eighty-five per cent of us are strongly against the opening of a Café Co coffee shop in our town. Yet plans are going ahead to build this café with alarming speed. I ask you, fellow residents, is this fair?

The Café Co chain is bland, soulless and dull. The only thing startling about it is its mediocrity. Unfortunately, its arrival will mean the end for our town's independent coffee shops.

This coffee shop chain is the bully of the playground. This bully will not rest until it has run its victims into the ground. This bully will not be satisfied until it has trampled over family businesses which have been nurtured and cherished for years.

This bully is powerful, but it can be stopped if we unite against it. Join me in the fight against Café Co today.

Language focus

1 Find examples of the following in the speech on page 68.

1 repetition of key words and phrases

2 use of specific examples to back up arguments

3 contrast

4 direct address (including the audience in the speech)

5 use of humour

6 a list of three adjectives

2 Consider each of the items in Exercise 1. What effect does their inclusion have on the speech overall?

3 Metaphors describe something by comparing it to something else which has the same qualities. Identify and explain the metaphor used in the speech.

Language note: emotive language

Writers use emotive language when they want to have an emotional impact on their readers, e.g. *alarming* and *trampled* in the speech you have just read. The words you use in your writing reflect your personal viewpoint. Consider, for example, the difference between the following three words to describe people who go to football matches: *supporters* (neutral), *fans* (positive) and *hooligans* (negative). The word you choose will have a great impact on the way your readers feel.

4 Underline the emotive words used in the speech. What effect do they have on its overall message?

5 Underline the emotive words in each sentence. What kind of speeches do they come from?

1 This is a proud and joyful day in the life of any father.

2 Furious mobs are rioting on the streets of our towns and cities.

3 All these years of toil and hard graft are behind us now!

4 As icy weather plunges our country into the coldest winter on record, we need people like you to volunteer!

5 See what the jewel in the crown of the Adriatic coast has to offer you.

6 Rewrite these sentences to make them more emotive.

1 Lottie and Leo are getting married after many years.

....

2 I would like to thank my teachers for all their support during my time at college.

....

3 I have enjoyed my years working in this department, but now it is time to retire.

....

4 There is a serious problem with litter in this town.

....

Looking closely

1 **Compare this speech to the one on page 68, then answer the questions.**

1 Why has this speech been written?

2 What emotions are being portrayed through the speaker's choice of words and phrasing?

3 Do you think the speech is effective?

When Vanessa first told me that I was making a speech at her wedding, I thought it was her way of getting back at me for accidentally dropping her expensive camera in the sea last year.

I have since realized what an honour it is to be asked to speak to you. You are the people that Vanessa and Alfred have invited to join their very special day. You have honoured them by coming along today, and touched us all with your generous gifts and contributions. You have made this day beautiful, lively and unforgettable.

As sister of the bride, I have been privileged to grow up with Vanessa. I had always wanted a little sister and when Vanessa arrived when I was five, I was not disappointed. She has the knack of bringing noise, hilarity and cheer to any situation. From the little girl who used to jump off walls dressed up as a butterfly, to the bigger girl who once decided to redecorate her bedroom using purple poster paints – Mum and Dad weren't too happy – my life with Vanessa has never been dull.

Many of you will know the details of how Vanessa and Alfred met – but for those of you who don't, let's just say it involved two hearts, two cars and my sister's curious inability to reverse park. If Vanessa found it strange when the man whose car she'd written off sent a huge bouquet of flowers to her house the day after – well, she certainly didn't say so. They've been together ever since, and I'm sure you all agree what a wonderful couple they make.

I hope you will all join me in wishing them a long, happy and eventful life together.

Language focus

1 **Find examples of the following in the speech:**

1 repetition of key words and phrases

2 use of specific examples to back up arguments

3 contrast

4 direct address (including the audience in the speech)

5 use of humour

6 a list of three adjectives

(2) Consider each of the items in Exercise 1. What effect does their inclusion have on the speech overall?

(3) Underline the emotive words used in the speech. What effect do they have on its overall message?

Useful tips

- Plan your speech carefully before you start writing. Outline the points you would like to cover and make sure you address them.
- Think about how you are going to open and close your speech. Your audience will remember a strong opening and a memorable conclusion.
- Write your speech out in full and then review it. Rewrite it and review it again until you are satisfied that your speech is clear and concise.
- Add humour where appropriate. This will help you to establish a good rapport with your audience.

Get writing

(1) You have been asked to give a speech at your sister's wedding. Talk about her personality and mention how she met her partner. Use humour and emotive language to move your audience and make your speech memorable.

(2) You are leaving your current job. Write a speech thanking your colleagues for all they have done for you and reflecting on what you have learned from working in this position.

(3) You are graduating from college, and you have been asked to write a speech on behalf of all your fellow students. In your speech, reflect on what you, as a cohort, have learned. Thank your teachers and look to the future. Make sure your speech is inspiring.

(4) A motorway is being built through your town and the council is proposing to demolish 50 houses in the area where you live. Write a speech to deliver to local residents at an emergency community meeting. You need to encourage the residents to take action.

Next steps

Find and watch speeches on YouTube. As you watch, think about the written text the speech has evolved from. What features of speech writing can you identify? Decide if the speech you are listening to has been well written and think about the reasons for your answer.

Choose one of the speeches you wrote in Get writing (above) and perform it to a friend. Ask for feedback, and on the basis of their feedback, rewrite your speech where necessary.

17 ADAPTING TO DIFFERENT AUDIENCES
Writing about yourself

Getting started

1 On what occasions might you write about yourself?
2 What level of formality is required by each occasion?
3 What other differences are there between the types of language required in these situations?

Looking closely

1 Read the four texts A–D. What do you know about Mayumi?

2 Identify Mayumi's reason for writing each text.

A .... C ....

B .... D ....

Text A

| Home | About | Gallery | Blog |

Mayumi Sato is a Japanese artist whose work is inspired by the beauty of the changing seasons in Hokkaido, where she lives and paints. Last year she received the Sasakwa Foundation prize for best young artist and her work has been exhibited at the Hokkaido Museum of Modern Art. When she is not painting, she leads art workshops for other young artists in her area.

Text B

For as long as I can remember, painting has been my passion and my release. It has allowed me to both fully appreciate and document the changes taking place in my natural environment. The constantly evolving landscape of Hokkaido has been central to my work. However, I believe my art would benefit from taking the opportunity to immerse myself in a different culture and landscape for a period of time. Studying for the Masters course in Fine Art at the Boston College of Art would enable me to grow as an artist and as a person.

Text C

Art Buddies wanted!

Hi! Thanks very much for reading my profile. I'm an art student called Mayumi and I'm new to the Boston area. I'm looking for like-minded people to explore this amazing city with. I love going to the movies, visiting art galleries and enhancing my shoe collection on a weekly basis! Hope to hear from you soon!

Text D

15th March

I can still remember our toboggan rides: our shrieks of pleasure tearing through the thick white blanket which covered the sleeping earth. We would often compete to see who could build the largest snowman, gathering sticks and stones from the nearby forest to make arms, eyes and noses. Although I didn't know it then, this was the closest I would ever feel to complete happiness.

Language focus

1 List the style, tone and register of each text.

2 Which text ...

  1 is written in the third person?   ......
  2 uses metaphor?   ......
  3 uses emotive language?   ......
  4 mentions professional achievements? ......
  5 talks about hobbies?   ......
  6 uses humour?   ......

3 Read the texts again and think about the intended audience. Who does Mayumi want to read each piece?

4 Each short text contains different information depending on the intended audience. Why has Mayumi done this?

5 Underline the irrelevant piece of information in each text. How could you make the text more relevant?

A

Jordan is a writer and photographer with a particular interest in island landscapes. His photo journal of a journey to the remote island of St Kilda won him a prestigious photography prize. He regularly contributes to The *Islander* online magazine. He has a great sense of humour.

B

Friendly, easy-going nurse in his mid-thirties seeks male and female friends to enjoy walks and relaxing times with. Loves the outdoors: camping, sunsets and mountain walks. Graduated with a degree in nursing five years ago. Looking forward to hearing from you!

C

Astronomy has always played a central role in my life. I also really enjoy flower arranging and meeting friends. Ever since I was a child the night sky has fascinated me, and this interest has continued throughout my school career. In my first year of high school I set up an astronomy club during the winter months. I also volunteer at my local observatory where I give talks to visiting school parties.

6 These sentences are either too formal or not formal enough for their intended readership. Rewrite them to make them more appropriate.

1 I've always been crazy about geology. [Personal statement for college application]

....

2 She is really into learning about second language acquisition. [Professional biography]

....

3 If you share my leisure interests then please do not hesitate to contact me. [Friendship website profile]

....

Language note: 'show, don't tell'

This advice is particularly important to bear in mind when you are writing about yourself. Rather than telling your reader you *are* something, you need to *show* it, by using examples and illustrations. This will also help you to avoid sounding egotistical. Compare:

Layla is an extremely hard-working person.

On top of running her own business, and editing Media Minds magazine, Layla also maintains her own photo blog.

7 Rewrite these sentences so that you are 'showing' rather than 'telling'.

1 My family were very poor when I was growing up.

....

2 I am extremely sociable and popular.

....

3 I am a really fun-loving person with a great sense of humour!

....

4 I am a very motivated student.

....

Useful tips

- Before you start writing, consider these questions: Who am I writing for?, What information should I include?, What tone should I use?
- Think about the length of your piece. Has a word count been stipulated? Professional biographies are usually very short (maximum 100 words).
- Reading samples of other people's work will give you an idea of the appropriate tone, length and style. For example, if you are writing a biography for your blog, visit other blogs similar to your own and read the biographies written there.
- Be yourself. Readers are quick to detect insincerity, so make sure that whatever you write reflects your true personality and experience.

Get writing

1 Your manager has asked you to write about yourself for the company website. In no more than 100 words describe your position, list your responsibilities and mention any achievements.

2 You have moved to Dublin, Ireland to work for a year. You are lonely at the weekend and would like to meet people who you can enjoy free time with. Write a short profile about yourself for a friendship website.

3 The university you are applying to has asked for a short personal statement, explaining why you want to study your subject. Write about yourself, focusing in particular on your subject and the importance it plays in your life.

Next steps

Write a short biography about yourself on your blog or social media page. Check it carefully (you may want to get feedback from a friend) before posting it.

Update your professional biography regularly. A little regular maintenance will help you to avoid having to redraft one completely in a couple of years' time.

18 ENGAGING YOUR READERS
Writing a blog post

Getting started

1 Make a list of the different types of blogs you visit.
2 What kind of blogs do you enjoy reading?
3 What have you noticed about the kind of writing you find on blogs? Think about language and level of formality.

Looking closely

1 Read Cécile's blog post. What three things does she love about life in the UK?

An Alien in London (Reflections of a young French woman)

| Home | About | Gallery |

Three things I've grown to love about life in the UK

Yesterday, my flatmates and I toasted the one-year anniversary of my arrival to this green and pleasant land (with a cup of milky tea and a soggy digestive biscuit, naturally!). It was an evening of reflection for me as I realized how things I found strange at first are now becoming almost second nature. Am I (gulp) becoming a Brit? Anyway, here's my top three things I've learned to love about life here. It would be great to hear more suggestions about delights I have maybe yet to discover!

1. Brit fashion

Before I left Paris I was under the impression that this was a bit of an oxymoron, but I'm not ashamed to admit I was wrong! Yes, the Brits may not be as carefully coiffed and as smartly co-ordinated as the French, but once your eyes adjust to crazy colour schemes and unorthodox skirt/ shoe combos you begin to take a certain pleasure in the eccentricity of it all. *Vive la différence!*

2. The British sweet tooth

Where we French have patisserie counters, the Brits have newsagents packed with sweets and bars of chocolates. How I pined for a real croissant in my first weeks here! Now I love nothing more than a family-sized bag of sugar-crusted cola cubes or a Double Decker (the chocolate bar, not that other great British icon, the red bus.)

3. The English language

Before coming here, learning the English language was an academic chore – mastering the lingua franca I needed to learn in order to succeed in life. Not being able to express myself fluently was a constant torture. Did I stand a slim chance (or even a fat chance) of succeeding in my studies? Yet, over the course of the year, I've begun to fall in love with the quirks and eccentricities of a language where words like shenanigans, japes and tomfoolery exist.

So here's to you, Great Brits! I'm looking forward to my next year here …

2 Why has Cécile written this blog post? Choose the best answer.

   a to provide travel advice to people visiting the UK for the first time

   b to persuade people to visit the UK

   c to reflect on her own experiences in the UK and entertain her readers

Language focus

1 Who do you think reads Cécile's blog? Consider the age, nationality and educational background of her target audience. Underline the words and phrases in the blog which helped you to choose your answer.

2 How do we know that Cécile wants people to comment on her blog post?

3 Which word best describes the tone of Cécile's blog post?

enthusiastic   affectionate   ironic

critical   reflective

4 What are the criticisms Cécile makes of the UK? How does she soften these observations to avoid sounding rude and negative?

5 Underline examples of these humorous devices in the blog post.

   1 onomatopoeia (where the sound of a word reflects the sound it describes)

   2 exaggeration

   3 wordplay

6 Read this extract from Jean-Claude's blog about British restaurants. What is the tone of this paragraph?

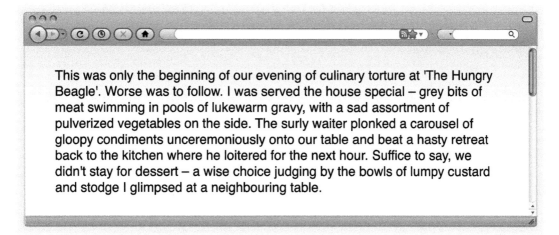

This was only the beginning of our evening of culinary torture at 'The Hungry Beagle'. Worse was to follow. I was served the house special – grey bits of meat swimming in pools of lukewarm gravy, with a sad assortment of pulverized vegetables on the side. The surly waiter plonked a carousel of gloopy condiments unceremoniously onto our table and beat a hasty retreat back to the kitchen where he loitered for the next hour. Suffice to say, we didn't stay for dessert – a wise choice judging by the bowls of lumpy custard and stodge I glimpsed at a neighbouring table.

7 Rewrite Jean-Claude's blog post by softening the tone so that it is less offensive and more humorous.

Language note: brackets

Brackets (or *parentheses*) are used to provide additional information in a piece of writing. The information contained in brackets can be omitted without changing the overall meaning of the sentence.

This was, perhaps, the most vibrant city I have ever visited (and I have seen many cities in my life).

Note that the full stop is placed at the end of the sentence (outside the bracket).

8 Why does Cécile use brackets in these sentences?

1 An Alien in London (Reflections of a young French woman)

2 My flatmates and I toasted the one-year anniversary of my arrival to this green and pleasant land (with a cup of milky tea and a soggy digestive biscuit, naturally!).

3 Am I (gulp) becoming a Brit?

4 Now I love nothing more than a family-sized bag of sugar-crusted cola cubes or a Double Decker (the chocolate bar, not that other great British icon, the red bus).

5 Did I stand a slim chance (or even a fat chance) of succeeding in my studies?

9 This blogger overuses brackets. What effect does this have?

After spending six months in London (how time flies when you're having fun!) I decided it was high time to venture north (and visit Scotland). I have always envisaged Scotland as a romantic land of myth, mist, castles and lakes, and wondered if the reality would live up to my dreams. Well, anyone who has ever arrived in Edinburgh (by train, anyway) will know that I was not disappointed. The sight of Castle Rock (where Edinburgh Castle is) filled me with excitement (and anticipation) about my stay in Scotland.

10 Rewrite the extract so that the blogger's meaning is clearer.

11 Read the following sentences from blog posts and insert brackets.

1 It can be difficult to persuade my son a complete computer fanatic to leave the house.

2 It was Ellie my personal trainer who finally inspired me to kick the habit.

3 She clearly wanted to go home not that I blamed her.

4 She's currently living in Skye a beautiful island off the west coast of Scotland.

5 Vienna or Becs as we call it in Hungarian is my favourite European city.

Useful tips

- Find your focus – who are your readers? What is your topic? Write about something you feel confident about. Some of the most popular blogs focus on everyday topics (for example, food and parenting).
- Be yourself – let your personality shine through your writing. Include your own feelings and opinions – a blog is not a report or an academic essay.
- Keep your paragraphs short (two or three sentences per paragraph). Blogs are read on screen so your content has to be as clear and accessible as possible.
- Address your readers directly. People are more likely to comment and visit your blog if you engage with your readers in this way.

Get writing

1. Write a blog post about your last English lesson for fellow English learners. What did you learn? What was challenging and what was easy? You can include links to useful sites.

2. Cécile uses the list format in her blog post. This is a popular way of structuring a blog post. Make a list of three things you like or dislike about something (*My three favourite films, Three things I like about learning English,* etc.). Write a short paragraph about each item on your list.

3. Think about something you know how to do well. Write a 'top tips' blog post on the subject. Remember to make your audience feel included in your post.

4. Write a blog post reviewing a film you have seen, a book you have read or a meal you have eaten. Focus on keeping your review descriptive but balanced.

Next steps

Surf the web for inspiring blogs and make a note of what you find. Which blogs get the most comments? How do they achieve this?

Many websites offer free blogging templates. Consider starting your own blog about a topic which inspires you. Spend time brainstorming ideas before you start to write.

19 SHARING NEWS AND INFORMATION
Writing for social media

Getting started

1 What different social media sites have you used this week?
2 What different purposes can you use social media sites for?
3 How does your social media writing style change depending on your purpose?

Looking closely

1 Read the texts and answer the questions below.

1 Identify each writer's purpose.

A ....
C ....
B ....
D ....

2 What type of social media sites would these appear on?

A ....
C ....
B ....
D ....

Text A

> Living in poverty is a reality for millions of women across the world. Educate yourself, educate others and take action. This year, International Female Poverty Awareness Day is on March 15.

Text B

> Techned@mperdu   1h
> Calling all #techie teachers! I'm giving an online workshop. Could you please say hello, where you come from and how often you use Twitter?

Text C

> LiliSzucs@liliszucs   2h
> Hey, have u got that Friday feeling? Fancy meeting up for dinner in Perth City with @joekale and @mchirier? #partytime

Text D

> Marie Pluhar
> 5 top tips for social media success. I've just returned from an inspiring weekend at the business and technology conference in Zurich. Great to network and put names to faces. My own personal highlight was Karl Jacob's talk on the topic above. Click here to read my summary.

Language note: social media sites

Although social media sites are generally quite relaxed, it is still important to write clearly and appropriately. Always proofread your work and use correct punctuation. Twitter may have a strict 140-character limit, but try to avoid using too many abbreviations. If you are struggling to fit your message into your Tweet, consider posting it elsewhere, for example on Facebook™ or your blog.

Language focus

1 How formal is the language used in texts A–D? Underline examples of semi-formal and informal language.

2 Look at how the writers have tried to make their posts engaging. Which posts …

1 ask questions? ……   **4** use humour?   ……   **6** link to further reading? ……

2 offer advice? ……   **5** use short sentences   ……   **7** use action verbs? ……

3 ask for help? ……

3 Read the posts and identify the target readers.

1 Going to see the new James Bond film tonight if anyone is interested in coming. #couldbefun

2 Went for a lovely meal last night. I had the lasagne and Simon ordered the roast chicken. It was really delicious.

3 I need help with my masters research. Could you please fill in this short survey and RT. Bit.ly.me6.vr

4 The local council are going to close our library. This is terrible, particularly as it is National Reading Week. We would be very grateful if you could sign our petition.

5 Fascinating post, as usual, Karl. I totaly agree with your point about air pollution – we have to do something quickly – the goverment can't be trusted to act on our behalf.

4 Do you think the posts are engaging? Explain why or why not.

5 Rewrite the posts in Exercise 3 to make them more engaging. Use the techniques from Exercise 2 to help you.

Looking closely

1 Read the advice about using Twitter. Are the sentences true or false? Write a tick in the correct place.

	True	False
1 You should use contractions and keep Tweets short.	…………	…………
2 A good Tweet is concise and unambiguous.	…………	…………
3 It is a good idea to use the passive voice in Tweets.	…………	…………
4 Offer suggestions and advice to your readers.	…………	…………
5 Use lots of capitalization – this will get you noticed.	…………	…………

2 Choose the best explanation a–d of what is happening in each of the Tweets below.

1	Cuts at local nursing home hit old folk hardest. Sign my petition: bit.ly.me/1Adfy0
2	Just blogged: 5 ways to get that promotion: bit.ly.fe/1chtx9
3	Just witnessed scary-looking lad give up his seat on bus for an old lady #heartwarming
4	So glad everyone had fun! RT Best dinner party ever with @julietal last night. Cheers Jules!

a uses the hashtag to sum up their own reaction to an event

b Retweets guest, adding her own short comment to acknowledge her guest's compliment

c uses a newspaper-style headline (active verbs, emotive language) to engage readers

d uses a list format to draw attention to a longer post

Language focus

1 Read Meilo's Tweets. What is she trying to do?

2 Decide what problems there might be with how she has written them.

3 Rewrite Meilo's Tweets to make them more appropriate, effective and engaging. Remember the 140-character limit.

Useful tips

- Think about the purpose of your writing before you decide which social media site to use. Consider having different goals for different social media sites. Use one to network professionally, and one to share news and interact with friends.
- Engage your readers by using images, quotes and video clips. Encourage interaction by asking questions. Don't be afraid to use humour as long as it is appropriate.
- Social media is about sharing. If you use it to constantly self-promote, and never respond to or acknowledge other people, don't expect to attract a large following.
- Be aware that employers regularly inspect the social media pages of potential employees. Try to keep your social and professional sites separate, and be careful about what you post.

Get writing

1. Think of a small business you would like to run, e.g. a cake shop or a web design company. Write five promotional Tweets to build up your customer base. Take care not to sound pushy. Keep your tone friendly and conversational.

2. Post a short update on Facebook to raise awareness about an important local or national event. Make sure your readers know why the event is important, when it is and what they need to do to participate.

3. Write a short summary of an interesting work event you have attended recently, and post it on a professional networking site. Make your account interesting and engaging, while maintaining the appropriate tone.

4. Write a post on a professional networking site in which you publicize a networking event you have planned. Make sure you include all the information which people will need to know, and make your event sound as attractive as possible.

Next steps

Give your social media presence a makeover. If you don't already blog, Tweet or write for an English-speaking audience, consider doing so. Many English learners write on social media sites, as writing in English will help you to reach a larger audience.

Connect with other people who write in English. Analyse the tone, language and content of posts you read. Note down the strategies which successful social media users employ, and bear this in mind in your own writing.

20 WRITING NOTES
Strategies for note taking

Getting started

1 In what different types of situations do you want or need to take notes?
2 What are the features of successful note taking?
3 How would you describe your own approach to taking notes?

Looking closely

1 **Read Lucy's notes and answer the questions.**

   1 What is the subject of the lecture she has attended?
   2 Are her notes clear? What kind of note-taking strategies has she used?

Ways mushrooms can save the world

1 Clean poll soils
mshrms absorb oil, become sat. with oils
Many mshrm forests dstryd but mshrms can b used 2 lead 2 habitat restoration
Exp - showed that 48 hrs reduced amt bacteria x 10,000

2 Making insecticides
mshrms can trap insects - nat. insecticide
Grp fungi that kill carpenter ants - now patented
Morphed culture in non-sporulating form
Non-sporulating = not reproducing
In exp. ants killed by mshrms - ants bcome mummified!

3 Treating illnesses
Mshrms can b used to trt illnesses, e.g. flu - flu a and flu b viruses and smallpox
We shld save the forest as matter of nat. defence against illness

4 Addressing energy crisis
N.B. mycelium = the long, thin body of a mshrm
Poss to generate econol from celluolose using mycelium as middle man
i.e. poss. solution 2 energy crisis?

Language focus

1 Look again at Lucy's notes and underline all of the abbreviations. What do her abbreviations mean?

Language note: abbreviations

When abbreviating words, note that it is easier to understand words which omit vowels than words which omit consonants. The kind of abbreviations used in texting, e.g. *4 = for*, are very useful when taking notes. You can also use your own personal abbreviations as long as you know they will make sense to you afterwards. Remember to write new words, e.g. *mycelium*, in full otherwise you might not understand your notes after the lecture.

---

2 Match the abbreviations to the words they represent.

1	s.o.	**a**	without
2	re:	**b**	very
3	diff	**c**	someone
4	sth	**d**	regarding
5	w/o	**e**	especially
6	esp	**f**	important
7	imp	**g**	something
8	v.	**h**	different / difficult

Language note: content words and function words

We can omit function words (such as articles, conjunctions, auxiliary verbs and prepositions) and still understand what we have written.

Mushrooms can trap insects – nat. insecticide

Lucy has left out the words *they are a* after the dash. We cannot usually omit content words (nouns, main verbs, adjectives and time phrases) without making our meaning much less clear.

---

3 Read the long sentences and write them in a shortened form. Make sure that you will be able to understand what you have written later.

1 Early childhood education creates better jobs and can therefore promote a stronger economy.

....

2 The microbes on your skin can help boost your immune system, while the microbes in your mouth can freshen your breath.

....

3 In recent years, the profile of the refugees has changed: they are younger, move mostly with their family and tend to emigrate for economic reasons.

....

Looking closely

1 Look at the three different approaches to note-taking. What are the advantages of each one? Do any of them have disadvantages?

1 The straightforward system as demonstrated on page 84.

2 If you know in advance what topics you will be making notes on, you can organize your notes into columns with headings.

Cleaning poltd. Soils	Making insecticides	Treating illnesses	Addressing energy crisis
Mshrms absorb oil, become sat. with oils Many mshrm forests destroyed	Mshrms can trap insects - nat. insecticide.	Mshrms can b used to trt illnesses, e.g. flu - flu a and flu b viruses and smallpox	N.B. Mycelium = the long, thin body of a mshrm
But -	Group of fungi that kill carpenter ants - this is now patented	We shld save the forest as matter of nat. defence against illness	Poss to generate econol from celluolose using mycelium as middle man l.e. Poss. olution 2 energy crisis?
Mhrms can be used to lead to habitat restoration	Morphed culture in non sporulating form		

3 You can also use a spidergram – note the main point in the centre of the page, and then write related ideas around the main point and smaller details underneath.

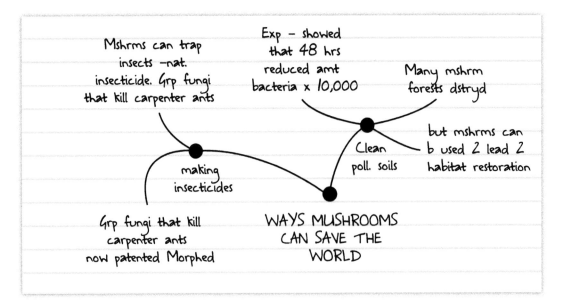

Language focus

1 Read the scenarios. Which note-taking strategy would use you in each case? Why?

1 You are studying for a philosophy exam. You are reading about Hegel's life and times.

2 You are taking notes at a talk on creativity in the workplace.

3 You are at a history lecture on the causes of the First World War.

Useful tips

- The strategies in this unit also work well when making notes from books.
- Make sure you revisit your notes shortly after you have written them. Check that your abbreviations still make sense to you, fill in any missing information and make sure that important words are spelled correctly.
- Have a look at the notes of a friend who has been to the same lecture as you. Exchange notes and see what you have missed.
- Don't file and forget your notes afterwards. Read them as soon after the lecture as possible and highlight any important points.

Get writing

1 Visit **www.collinselt.com/englishforlife/extras** and listen to a lecture about the history of science. Which of the four note-taking strategies will you use? Listen and make notes.

2 Now listen to another extract from the same lecture. Make notes again, but try a different note-taking strategy this time. Was this approach more or less successful?

3 Read a chapter of an academic or reference book. Take notes, using one of the note-taking strategies from this unit.

Next steps

It is well worth practising note taking at home. Search for a subject which interests you along with the word "lecture" on YouTube and see what comes up. Use one of the note-taking strategies from this unit while you listen. Revisit your notes after a couple of days. How useful are they?

APPENDIX 1 – Useful phrases

1 Informal emails

Salutations	Closing expressions	Signing off
Hey!	Well, got to go now.	Love
Hi!	Give my love to …	Lots of love
	Say hello to …	
	See you soon!	

2 Formal emails and letters

Salutations

Dear…
Dear Sir / Madam
Dear Sir or Madam
Dear Mr / Mrs / Miss [family name]

Giving a reason for writing

I am writing with regard to …
I am writing in relation to …
I am writing to enquire / ask about

Asking for information

I would be grateful if …
I wonder if you could …
Could you …?
I would particularly like to know …
I would be interested in having more details about …

Introducing a topic

As I am sure you will be aware, …
It has come to my attention that …

Requesting action

… should be addressed as a matter of urgency.
I would like to request that …
Your prompt attention to this matter would be greatly appreciated.
I wonder if you could …

Complaining

I am writing to express my concern about …
This has come as a great shock to me, as I have always admired your …
I am writing to express my deep disappointment with regard to …
I am afraid that … failed to live up to my expectations.
I would like to be refunded for …
I would really appreciate a reply within the next two weeks.
I would also appreciate your reassurance that this will not happen again.

Writing a reference

It is a pleasure to support Kate's application unreservedly.
Should you require any further information please do not hesitate to contact me.
I have a very high opinion of Kate's academic and personal qualities.
I am writing to recommend Kate for employment.

Writing a covering letter

I am writing in reply to the advertisement on your website for the post of … at …
As my CV illustrates …
Thank you for your time in reading this letter. I look forward to hearing from you.

Writing for a cause you believe in

I was very concerned to read about …
I understand that …
It has come to my attention that …
Please use your influence and authority to ensure …
Please ensure that …
I look forward to hearing from you on this important matter.
I would be grateful if you could confirm that your company does indeed oppose such practices.
Please can you confirm that you have taken steps to address …

The layout of a formal letter follows strict conventions. It is important to include your name and address, the recipient's name and address, the date you are writing, and a formal salutation and sign off.

7 Abbey Gate
Leicester
LE4 3TS

Leicester City Council
New Walk Centre
Leicester
LE1 6ZG

23 May

Dear Mayor Soulsby,

I am writing with regard to my concern about the lack of safe pedestrian walkways and cycle paths in this city. As a mother of two school-age children, I feel that the road traffic situation as it stands is extremely dangerous and should be addressed as a matter of urgency.

As I am sure you will be aware, there has been an increasing number of road accidents in the past two years. Despite the considerable amount of money which has been poured into financing road safety campaigns in schools, the situation is not improving. What needs to be remedied is the complete lack of wide pavements and dedicated cycle areas so that children (and adults) can travel to school and work safely.

I would like to request that this issue be addressed in your transport strategy. Your prompt attention to this matter would be greatly appreciated.

Yours sincerely,

A. Harrison

Ayla Hassan

APPENDIX 3 – Phrasal verbs and their formal equivalents

These phrasal verbs all appear in this book. Here are their formal equivalents:

back up: support

build up: increase gradually

check something out: look at something which seems interesting

come across: discover

come back: return

close down: shut

dash out: leave quickly

do up: decorate

fill in: complete

get about: travel around

get along: have a friendly relationship

get back at someone: do something to upset or annoy someone after they have upset or annoyed you

get off (without): escape (humorous)

give up: stop doing something

go ahead: continue

go through: be passed (for example a law)

lay on for someone: provide

leave out: omit

pick up (a job): find

point out: indicate

pull out: depart (for example a bus)

pull off: remove

be put out by something: be inconvenienced by something or someone

run something past someone: propose something

set up: found

speed up: accelerate

take something out: remove

turn into: become

work out: discover

APPENDIX 4 – Proofreading

Proofreading is very important to ensure that your work does not contain any spelling, grammar or typographical errors. Proofreading comes at the very end of the writing process. By the time you come to proofread your work, you will already have reviewed and edited it, so the errors you are looking for will typically be small ones.

How to proofread

- If possible, leave your writing for a few days before reading it. You will find it far easier to spot mistakes if there is a little distance between you and your work.
- Find a quiet, uncluttered place to sit. Switch off your music – proofreading demands concentration.
- Read your work aloud. This will make sure you focus on every word you have written. You will also have the opportunity to hear how your work sounds.

As you read ...

- rewrite any sentences or phrases you stumble over. Perhaps your punctuation is incorrect in these cases.
- be wary of the spellchecker on your computer. It can tell you if you have misspelled *accommodation*, for example, but it will not pick up on wrong words, e.g. if you write *bear* instead of *bare*. Use your dictionary to help you here.
- check for repetition. Do you keep repeating the same word? If so, use a thesaurus to help you find synonyms. Do all your sentences begin the same way? In that case, vary your sentence structure.

Why not try ...

- writing your own personal checklist of the mistakes you know you are most likely to make? Refer to this as you read through your work.
- asking a friend or colleague to proofread your work too. A fresh pair of eyes will almost always spot things you haven't noticed.

The most difficult words from the units are defined here in this mini-dictionary. The definitions are extracts from the Collins COBUILD Advanced Dictionary and focus on the meanings of the words in the context in which they appear in the book.

Unit 1

alert VERB If you **alert** someone **to** a situation, especially a dangerous or unpleasant situation, you tell them about it. • *He wanted to alert people to the activities of the group.*

amenity N-COUNT **Amenities** are things such as shopping centres or sports facilities that are provided for people's convenience, enjoyment, or comfort. • *The hotel amenities include health clubs, conference facilities, and banqueting rooms.*

awesome ADJ An **awesome** person or thing is extremely good. [INFORMAL] • *It was an awesome game!*

considerable ADV **Considerable** means great in amount or degree. [FORMAL] • *Doing it properly makes considerable demands on our time.*

expertise N-COUNT **Expertise** is special skills or knowledge that is acquired by training, study, or practice. • *The problem is that most local authorities lack the expertise to deal sensibly in this market.*

inconvenience N-VAR If someone or something causes **inconvenience**, they cause problems or difficulties. • *We apologize for any inconvenience caused during the repairs.*

jaunt N-COUNT A **jaunt** is a short journey which you go on for pleasure or excitement. • *The girls had returned from their jaunt into the town.*

mutual ADJ You use **mutual** to describe a situation, feeling, or action that is experienced, felt, or done by both of two people mentioned.

• *The East and the West can work together for their mutual benefit and progress.* **mutually** ADV • *Attempts to reach a mutually agreed solution had been fruitless.*

refurbishment N-UNCOUNT The **refurbishment** of something is the act or process of cleaning it, decorating it, and providing it with new equipment or facilities. • *The hotel had been closed for a year while major refurbishment took place.*

Unit 2

dedicated ADJ You use **dedicated** to describe something that is made, built, or designed for one particular purpose or thing. • *Such areas should also be served by dedicated cycle routes.*

pour VERB If something – such as information – **pours** into a place, a lot of it is obtained or given. • *Martin, 78, died yesterday. Tributes poured in from around the globe.*

prompt ADJ If you are **prompt** to do something, you do it without delay or you are not late. • *You have been so prompt in carrying out all these commissions.*

remedy VERB If you **remedy** something that is wrong or harmful, you correct it or improve it. • *A great deal has been done internally to remedy the situation.*

resign VERB If you **resign** from a job or position, you formally announce that you are leaving it. • *A hospital administrator has resigned over claims he lied to get the job.*

urgent ADJ If something is **urgent**, it needs to be dealt with as soon as possible. • *There is an urgent need for food and water.* • *He had urgent business in New York.* **urgency** • *It is a matter of utmost urgency.*

Unit 3

bill N-COUNT In government, a **bill** is a formal statement of a proposed new law that is discussed and then voted on. • *The bill was approved by a large majority.*

collective ADJ **Collective** actions, situations, or feelings involve or are shared by every member of a group of people. • *It was a collective decision.*

enforce VERB If people in authority **enforce** a law or a rule, they make sure that it is obeyed, usually by punishing people who do not obey it. • *Until now, the government has only enforced the ban with regard to American ships.*

intimidate VERB If you **intimidate** someone, you deliberately make them frightened enough to do what you want them to do. • *Attempts to intimidate people into voting for the governing party did not work.* **intimidation** NOUN • *...an inquiry into allegations of intimidation during last week's vote.*

lousy ADJ If you describe something as **lousy**, you mean that it is of very bad quality or that you do not like it. [INFORMAL] • *He blamed Fiona for a lousy weekend.*

penalize VERB If a person or group is **penalized** for something, they are made to suffer in some way because of it. • *Some of the players may, on occasion, break the rules and be penalised.*

scrap VERB If you **scrap** something, you get rid of it or cancel it. [INFORMAL] • *President Hussein called on all countries in the Middle East to scrap nuclear or chemical weapons.*

skip VERB If you **skip** something that you usually do or something that most people do, you decide not to do it. • *It is important not to skip meals.*

sniff VERB If you **sniff** something or sniff at it, you smell it by sniffing. • *Suddenly, he stopped and sniffed the air.*

Unit 4

blabber VERB If someone **blabbers**, they talk a lot, especially about things that are not very important. [INFORMAL] • *He blabbered on and on about his private life.*

efficacious ADJ Something that is **efficacious** is effective. [FORMAL] • *The nasal spray was new on the market and highly efficacious.*

IMHO PHRASE **IMHO** is the written abbreviation for 'in my humble opinion', mainly used in text messages and e-mails. • *Something like this is just (IMHO) wrong.*

inane ADJ If you describe someone's behaviour or actions as **inane**, you think they are very silly or stupid. • *He always had this inane grin.*

incessant ADJ An **incessant** process or activity is one that continues without stopping. • *…incessant rain.* **incessantly** ADV • *Dee talked incessantly.*

malfunction VERB If a machine or part of the body **malfunctions**, it fails to work properly. • *There must have been a computer malfunction.*

shirk VERB If someone does not **shirk** their responsibility or duty, they do what they have a responsibility to do. • *The Government will not shirk from considering the need for further action.*

Unit 5

articulate ADJ If you describe someone as **articulate**, you mean that they are able to express their thoughts and ideas easily and well. • *She is an articulate young woman.*

conscientious ADJ Someone who is **conscientious** is very careful to do their work properly. • *We are generally very conscientious about our work.*

diligent ADJ Someone who is **diligent** works hard in a careful and thorough way. • *Meyers is a diligent and prolific worker.*

dishevelled ADJ If you describe someone's hair, clothes, or appearance as **dishevelled**, you mean that it is very untidy. • *She arrived flushed and dishevelled.*

focused ADJ If you describe someone or something as **focused**, you approve of the fact that they have a clear and definite purpose. • *I spent the next year just wandering. I wasn't focused.*

innovative ADJ An **innovative** person introduces changes and new ideas. • *He was one of the most creative and innovative engineers of his generation.*

prestigious ADJ A **prestigious** institution, job, or activity is respected and admired by people. • *It's one of the best equipped and most prestigious schools in the country.*

resourceful ADJ Someone who is **resourceful** is good at finding ways of dealing with problems. • *He was amazingly inventive and resourceful, and played a major role in my career.*

unreserved ADJ An **unreserved** opinion or statement is one that expresses a feeling or opinion completely and without any doubts. • *Charles displays unreserved admiration for his grandfather.* **unreservedly** ADV • *We apologize unreservedly for any imputation of incorrect behaviour by Mr Taylor.*

utterly ADV You use **utterly** to emphasise that something is very great in extent, degree, or amount.• *The new laws coming in are utterly ridiculous.*

Unit 6

adaptable ADJ If you describe a person or animal as adaptable, you mean that they are able to change their ideas or behaviour in order to deal with new situations. • *… a more adaptable and skilled workforce.* **adaptability** NOUN • *The adaptability of wool is one of its great attractions.*

adept ADJ Someone who is **adept** at something can do it skilfully. • *He's usually very adept at keeping his private life out of the media.*

avid ADJ You use **avid** to describe someone who is very enthusiastic about something that they do. • *He misses not having enough books because he's an avid reader.*

deadline N-COUNT A **deadline** is a time or date before which a particular task must be finished or a particular thing must be done. • *We were not able to meet the deadline because of manufacturing delays.*

hone VERB If you **hone** something, for example a skill, technique, idea, or product, you carefully develop it over a long period of time so that it is exactly right for your purpose. • *Leading companies spend time and money on honing the skills of senior managers.*

relish VERB If you **relish** the idea, thought, or prospect of something, you are looking forward to it very much. • *Jacqueline is not relishing the prospect of another spell in prison.*

relocate VERB If people or businesses **relocate** or if someone relocates them, they move to a different place.• *If the company was to relocate, most employees would move.*

shrewd ADJ A **shrewd** person is able to understand and judge a situation quickly and to use this understanding to their own advantage. • *She's a shrewd businesswoman.*

Unit 7

airbrush VERB To **airbrush** a photograph or other image means to change it using an airbrush, especially to make it more beautiful or perfect. • *... bits of photographs cut, pasted and then airbrushed to create a convincing whole.*

cosset VERB If someone is **cosseted**, everything possible is done for them and they are protected from anything unpleasant. • *Our kind of travel is definitely not suitable for people who expect to be cosseted.*

delusion N-COUNT A **delusion** is a false idea. • *I was under the delusion that he intended to marry me.*

devote VERB If you **devote** yourself, your time, or your energy to something, you spend all or most of your time or energy on it. • *He decided to devote the rest of his life to scientific investigation.*

endure VERB If you **endure** a painful or difficult situation, you experience it and do not avoid it or give up, usually because you cannot. • *The company endured heavy financial losses.*

hardship N-VAR **Hardship** is a situation in which your life is difficult or unpleasant, • *One of the worst hardships is having so little time to spend with one's family.*

hover VERB If you **hover**, you stay in one place and move slightly in a nervous way, for example because you cannot decide what to do. • *Judith was hovering in the doorway.*

loom VERB If a worrying or threatening situation or event is **looming**, it seems likely to happen soon. • *The threat of renewed civil war looms ahead.*

resilient ADJ People and things that are **resilient** are able to recover easily and quickly from unpleasant or damaging events. • *When the U.S. stock market collapsed in October 1987, the Japanese stock market was the most resilient.*

scrutiny N-UNCOUNT If a person or thing is under **scrutiny**, they are being studied or observed very carefully. • *His private life came under media scrutiny.*

Unit 8

chuck VERB When you **chuck** something somewhere, you throw it there in a casual or careless way. • *I took a great dislike to the clock, so I chucked it in the dustbin.*

drip VERB When liquid drips somewhere, or you **drip** it somewhere, it falls in individual small drops. • *Sit your child forward and let the blood drip into a tissue or on to the floor.*

panel N-COUNT A **panel** is a flat rectangular piece of wood or other material that forms part of a larger object such as a door. • *... the frosted glass panel set in the centre of the door.*

plonk VERB If you **plonk** something somewhere, you put it or drop it there heavily and carelessly. [BRIT, INFORMAL] • *She plonked the beer on the counter.*

squabble VERB When people **squabble**, they quarrel about something that is not really important. • *My four-year-old squabbles with his friends.*

twiddle VERB If you **twiddle** something, you twist it or turn it quickly with your fingers. • *He twiddled a knob on the dashboard.*

Unit 9

buckle VERB If an object **buckles** or if something buckles it, it becomes bent as a result of very great heat or force. • *A freak wave had buckled the deck.*

deluge N-COUNT A **deluge** is a sudden, very heavy fall of rain. • *About a dozen homes were damaged in the deluge.*

gutted ADJ If you are **gutted**, you feel extremely disappointed or depressed about something that has happened. [BRIT, INFORMAL] • *Birmingham City supporters will be absolutely gutted if he leaves the club.*

lug VERB If you **lug** a heavy or awkward object somewhere, you carry it there with difficulty. [INFORMAL] • *Nobody wants to lug around huge suitcases full of clothes.*

overflow N-COUNT An **overflow** is a hole or pipe through which liquid can flow out of a container when it gets too full.

remnant N-COUNT The **remnants** of something are small parts of it that are left over when the main part has disappeared or been destroyed. • *Beneath the present church were remnants of Roman flooring.*

rummage VERB If you **rummage** through something, you search for something you want by moving things around in a careless or hurried way. • *They rummage through piles of second hand clothes for something that fits.*

tank N-COUNT A **tank** is a large container for holding liquid or gas. • *...an empty fuel tank.*

Unit 10

attention to detail PHRASE **Attention to detail** is when you are careful to make sure that everything is correct. • *This work demands great patience and attention to detail.*

dynamic ADJ If you describe someone as **dynamic**, you approve of them because they are full of energy or full of new and exciting ideas. • *He seemed a dynamic and energetic leader.*

overpriced ADJ If you say that something is **overpriced**, you mean that you think it costs much more than it should. • *Any property which does not sell within six weeks is overpriced.*

stamina N-UNCOUNT **Stamina** is the physical or mental energy needed to do a tiring activity for a long time. • *You have to have a lot of stamina to be a top-class dancer.*

unflagging ADJ If you describe something such as support, effort, or enthusiasm as **unflagging**, you mean that it does not stop or get less as time passes. • *He was sustained by the unflagging support of his family.*

Unit 11

abrupt ADJ Someone who is **abrupt** speaks in a rather rude, unfriendly way. • *He was abrupt to the point of rudeness.*

anticipate VERB If an event, especially a cultural event, is eagerly **anticipated**, people expect that it will be very good, exciting, or interesting. • *... the most eagerly anticipated rock event of the year.*

compensation N-UNCOUNT **Compensation** is money that someone who has experienced loss or suffering claims from the person or organisation responsible, or from the state. • *The Court ordered Dr Williams to pay £300 compensation and £100 costs after admitting assault.*

detritus N-UNCOUNT **Detritus** is the small pieces of rubbish that remain after an event has finished or when something has been used. [INFORMAL] • *... the detritus of war.*

half-baked ADJ If you describe an idea or plan as **half-baked**, you mean that it has not been properly thought out, and so is stupid or impractical. • *This is another half-baked scheme that isn't going to work.*

lukewarm ADJ Something, especially a liquid, that is **lukewarm** is only slightly warm. • *The coffee was weak and lukewarm.*

misleading ADJ If you describe something as **misleading**, you mean that it gives you a wrong idea or impression. • *The article contains several misleading statements.*

readily ADV If you do something **readily**, you do it in a way which shows that you are very willing to do it. • *I asked her if she would allow me to interview her, and she readily agreed.*

shoddy ADJ **Shoddy** work or a shoddy product has been done or made carelessly or badly. • *I'm normally quick to complain about shoddy service.*

Unit 12

butterfingers N-SING A **butterfingers** is a person who often drops things. [INFORMAL] • *Fabien is the ultimate butterfingers.*

casualty N-COUNT A **casualty** of a particular event or situation is a person or a thing that has suffered badly as a result of that event or situation. • *Fiat has been one of the greatest casualties of the recession.*

crockery N-UNCOUNT **Crockery** is the plates, cups, saucers, and dishes that you use at meals. • *We had no fridge, cooker, cutlery or crockery.*

resume VERB If you **resume** an activity or if it resumes, it begins again. [FORMAL] • *The search is expected to resume early today.*

shipshape ADJ If something is **shipshape**, it looks tidy, neat, and in good condition. • *The house only needs an occasional coat of paint to keep it shipshape.*

taunt VERB If someone **taunts** you, they say unkind or insulting things to you, especially about your weaknesses or failures. • *A gang taunted a disabled man.*

transfer VERB If you **transfer** money, you move it from one bank account to another. • *transferred some money from my business account to my personal account.*

withhold VERB If you **withhold** something that someone wants, you do not let them have it. [FORMAL] • *The captain decided to withhold the news from his officers.*

Unit 13

defenceless ADJ If someone or something is **defenceless**, they are weak and unable to defend themselves properly. • *It was a horrific attack on a defenceless old woman.*

despicable ADJ If you say that a person or action is **despicable**, you are emphasizing that they are extremely nasty, cruel, or evil. • *The Minister said the bombing was a despicable crime.*

finite ADJ Something that is **finite** has a definite fixed size or extent. [formal] • *The fossil fuels (coal and oil) are finite resources.*

flabbergasted ADJ If you say that you are **flabbergasted**, you are emphasizing that you are extremely surprised. • *Everybody was flabbergasted when I announced I was going to emigrate to Australia.*

footage N-UNCOUNT **Footage** of a particular event is a film of it or the part of a film which shows this event. • *They are planning to show exclusive footage from this summer's festivals.*

luxuriate VERB If you **luxuriate** in something, you relax in it and enjoy it very much, especially because you find it comfortable and luxurious. • *Ralph was luxuriating in the first real holiday he'd had in years.*

plunder VERB If someone **plunders** a place or plunders things from a place, they steal things from it. • *This has been done by plundering £4 billion from the Government reserves.*

pulp N-UNCOUNT **Pulp** is a soft substance that is made by crushing something, especially wood. • *Forest products include pulp and timber.*

Unit 14

balmy ADJ **Balmy** weather is fairly warm and pleasant. • *... a balmy summer's evening.*

dash VERB If you **dash** somewhere, you run or go there quickly and suddenly. • *Suddenly she dashed down to the cellar.*

gaggle N-COUNT You can use **gaggle** to refer to a group of people, especially if they are noisy or disorganized. • *A gaggle of journalists sit in a hotel foyer waiting impatiently.*

gaunt ADJ If someone looks **gaunt**, they look very thin, usually because they have been very ill or worried. • *Looking gaunt and tired, he denied there was anything to worry about.*

stroll N-COUNT A **stroll** is a slow, relaxed walk. • *After dinner, I took a stroll around the city.*

muster VERB If you **muster** something such as support, strength, or energy, you gather as much of it as you can in order to do something. • *He travelled around West Africa trying to muster support for his movement.*

peer VERB If you **peer** at something, you look at it very hard, usually because it is difficult to see clearly. • *I had been peering at a computer print-out that made no sense at all.*

shuffle VERB If you **shuffle** somewhere, you walk there without lifting your feet properly off the ground. • *Moira shuffled across the kitchen.*

slave over VERB If you say that a person is **slaving over** something or is slaving for someone, you mean that they are working very hard. • *When you're busy all day the last thing you want to do is spend hours slaving over a hot stove.*

stifling ADJ **stifling** heat is so intense that it makes you feel uncomfortable. You can also use stifling to describe a place that is extremely hot. • *The stifling heat of the little room was beginning to make me nauseous.*

Unit 15

grunt VERB If you **grunt**, you make a low sound, especially because you are annoyed or not interested in something. • *He grunted his thanks.*

infinite ADJ If you describe something as **infinite**, you are emphasizing that it is extremely great in amount or degree. • *... an infinite variety of landscapes.* • *The choice is infinite.* **Infinitely** ADV • *His design was infinitely better than anything I could have done.*

leg N-COUNT A **leg** of a long journey is one part of it, usually between two points where you stop. • *The first leg of the journey was by boat to Lake Naivasha in Kenya.*

perspiration N-UNCOUNT **Perspiration** is the liquid which comes out on the surface of your skin when you are hot or frightened. [INFORMAL] • *His hands were wet with perspiration.*

remarkable ADJ Someone or something that is **remarkable** is unusual or special in a way that makes people notice them and be surprised or impressed. • *He was a remarkable man.* **remarkably** • *The Scottish labour market has been remarkably successful in absorbing the increase in the number of graduates.*

stream VERB If a liquid **streams** somewhere, it flows or comes out in large amounts. • *Tears streamed down their faces.*

Unit 16

bland ADJ If you describe someone or something as **bland**, you mean that they are rather dull and unexciting. • *... a bland, 12-storey office block.*

curious ADJ If you describe something as **curious**, you mean that it is unusual or difficult to understand. • *The pageant promises to be a curious mixture of the ancient and modern.*

hilarity N-UNCOUNT **Hilarity** is great amusement and laughter.

knack N-COUNT A **knack** is a particularly clever or skilful way of doing something successfully, especially something which most people find difficult. • *He's got the knack of getting people to listen.*

reverse VERB When a car **reverses** or when you reverse it, the car is driven backwards. • *Another car reversed out of the drive.*

startling ADJ Something that is **startling** is so different, unexpected, or remarkable that people react to it with surprise. • *... startling new evidence.*

trample VERB To **trample** on someone's rights or values or to trample them means to deliberately ignore them. • *Diplomats denounced the leaders for trampling their citizens' civil rights.*

Unit 17

contribute VERB If you **contribute** to a magazine, newspaper, or book, you write things that are published in it. • *I was asked to contribute to a newspaper article making predictions for the new year.*

evolve VERB If something **evolves** or you evolve it, it gradually develops over a period of time into something different and usually more advanced. • ...a tiny airline which eventually evolved into Pakistan International Airlines.

immerse VERB If you **immerse** yourself in something that you are doing, you become completely involved in it. • Since then I've lived alone and immersed myself in my career.

landscape N-VAR The **landscape** is everything you can see when you look across an area of land, including hills, rivers, buildings, trees, and plants. • We moved to Northamptonshire and a new landscape of hedges and fields.

lead VERB If you **lead** a group of people, an organization, or an activity, you are in control or in charge of the people or the activity. • Mr Mendes was leading a campaign to save Brazil's rainforest from exploitation.

workshop N-COUNT A **workshop** is a period of discussion or practical work on a particular subject in which a group of people share their knowledge or experience. • Trumpeter Marcus Belgrave ran a jazz workshop for young artists.

Unit 18

gulp VERB if you **gulp**, you swallow air, often making a noise in your throat as you do so, because you are nervous or excited.• I gulped, and then proceeded to tell her the whole story.

jape N-COUNT a **jape** is a silly trick that you play on someone which is quite funny and which does not really involve upsetting them.

loiter VERB if you **loiter** somewhere, you remain there or walk up and down without any real purpose. • Unemployed young men loiter at the entrance of the factory.

pine VERB if you **pine** for something, you want it very much, especially when it is unlikely that you will be able to have it. • I pine for the countryside.

shenanigans N-PLURAL you can use **shenanigans** to refer to rather dishonest or immoral behaviour, especially when you think it is amusing or interesting. [INFORMAL] • ... the private shenanigans of public figures.

soggy ADJ something that is **soggy** is unpleasantly wet. • ... soggy cheese sandwiches.

surly ADJ someone who is **surly** behaves in a rude bad-tempered way. • He became surly and rude towards me.

tomfoolery N-UNCOUNT **tomfoolery** is playful behaviour, usually of a rather silly, noisy, or rough kind. • Were you serious, or was that a bit of tomfoolery?

Unit 19

BOGOF PHRASE **BOGOF** is the abbreviation of 'Buy one get one free', used in marketing and shops for saying that if a customer buys a product they will get another of the same product free. • A lot of customers take advantage of BOGOF deals.

fancy VERB If you **fancy** something, you want to have it or to do it. [INFORMAL] • What do you fancy doing, anyway?

highlight N-COUNT The **highlights** of an event, activity, or period of time are the most interesting or exciting parts of it. • ... a match that is likely to prove one of the highlights of the tournament.

inspiring ADJ Something or someone that is **inspiring** is exciting and makes you feel strongly interested and enthusiastic... • She was one of the most inspiring people I've ever met.

petition N-COUNT A **petition** is a document signed by a lot of people which asks a government or other official group to do a particular thing. • We recently presented the government with a petition signed by 4,500 people.

poverty N-UNCOUNT **Poverty** is the state of being extremely poor. • According to World Bank figures, 41 per cent of Brazilians live in absolute poverty.

Unit 20

absorb VERB If something **absorbs** a liquid, gas, or other substance, it soaks it up or takes it in. • Plants absorb carbon dioxide from the air and moisture from the soil.

habitat N-VAR The **habitat** of an animal or plant is the natural environment in which it normally lives or grows. • In its natural habitat, the hibiscus will grow up to 25ft.

mummify VERB If a dead body is **mummified**, it is preserved, for example by rubbing it with special oils and wrapping it in cloth. • In America, people are paying up to $150,000 to be mummified after death.

patent VERB If you **patent** something, you obtain a patent for it. • He patented the idea that the atom could be split.

promote VERB If people **promote** something, they help or encourage it to happen, increase, or spread. • You don't have to sacrifice environmental protection to promote economic growth.

restoration N-UNCOUNT **Restoration** is the act or process of returning something to the good condition that it was in before. • Conservationists are working forest restoration projects.

ANSWER KEY

Unit 1   Writing emails

Looking closely

1

In the first email, the writer is clearly good friends with the recipient. In the second email, it's possible that the writer has never met the person he is writing to.

Language focus

1

The first email is informal.

Sample answers:

Hey, how are things, in ages, guessing you've been busy, jaunt, fancy doing, bang in the middle of town, dead handy, done it up, awesome, fair bit, what do you reckon

The second email is semi-formal.

Sample answers:

Dear, I hope you are well, we were hoping, accommodate, location, within easy walking distance, I think I mentioned, a little need of refurbishment, I hope that this will not inconvenience you, I'm really looking forward to hearing from you

2

1 I'm going to	4 would you like to …?
2 right in the centre of	5 fantastic
3 very convenient	

3

Sample answers:

1   I've recently refurbished my flat.
2   I have a proposal I would like to make to you.
3   You would be able to travel around, even without a car.

4

1   Our flat needs doing up.
2   I hope this won't put you out too much.
3   Are you planning to check out the Rijksmuseum?

Looking closely

1

The writer probably does not know the lecturer he is writing to, although they may well have corresponded by email in the past. However, he is writing in a professional capacity. Using a less formal style might be perceived as showing a lack of respect for his colleague.

Language focus

1

1 c		2 a		3 d		4 b	

2

Sample answers:

absolutely delighted that you have accepted our invitation, We are very much looking forward to, Knowing your considerable subject expertise, In answer to your question, the duration of your stay, situated, amenities, Please do not hesitate to contact me should you require any further information, Kind regards

3

1   contact me / further
2   on
3   enquire
4   grateful / appropriate / complete

Get writing

1

Sample answer:

Dear Lucy,

How are things with you? Sorry it's taken me so long to get in touch!

Thanks very much for your email – I am indeed heading to London this autumn. Maybe I could pop in and see you? If you could let me know how you are fixed during the first week of October that'd be great.

See you soon,

Francesco

2

Sample answer:

Dear Aunt Tabitha,

I hope you are well. I was absolutely delighted to receive your email and to hear all your news about New Zealand. It looks like a beautiful place.

How kind of you to ask me to visit. I would love to! Please let me know which dates suit you best and I will start planning my travel itinerary.

With much love,

Fay

3

Sample answer:

Hey,

Are you still up for a trip somewhere this summer? I've just found these amazing deals for Budapest. Check out the pictures online – it looks totally awesome.

There are loads of beautiful buildings and museums, and best of all some thermal baths where we can just hang out and relax for hours. We could stay in a hostel, so it shouldn't be too expensive.

Do you fancy it?

Gemma

Unit 2   Writing letters

Looking closely

1

1   The writer is writing to complain about the lack of pedestrian and cycling facilities in her city. She wants the mayor to use his power and influence to do something about the problem.

2   The writer may think that a formal letter is more likely to get noticed than an email.

3   The language used in a letter is often more formal.

4   The layout of a letter is stricter than in an email – there are certain guidelines that should always be followed.

Language focus

1

the traffic situation should be addressed, money which has been poured into financing road safety campaigns, what needs to be remedied is, this issue be addressed, would be greatly appreciated

The use of the passive voice makes the letter more polite and less aggressive. Compare *should be addressed* with *you should address*.

2

1   correct

2   I narrowly avoided being run down on my way home from work last night.

3   correct

4   Your presence at the meeting would be greatly appreciated

3

extremely, greatly

4

1   extremely   3   most   5   highly

2   deeply   4   great

Looking closely

1

1   The writer is resigning from her job.

2   She probably feels that a written letter has more of a sense of occasion than an email.

3   The letter is a little less formal. This is because she knows her boss. However, the level of formality lends it a sufficient amount of professionalism.

Language focus

1

While being

2

1   While understanding your reasons for leaving, I am very sorry to see you go.

2   Before writing the report, I made sure I had done sufficient reading.

3   In choosing to work at this company, I made a great career decision.

4   By writing to you, I am hoping to raise awareness of this situation.

3

I am writing to inform you, Please accept my sincere thanks, Yours sincerely

4

1   I would be grateful for a reply at your earliest convenience.

2   I am writing to express my concern about …

3   I am writing in relation to …

4   Thank you for your time and consideration.

5

Sample answer:

Dear Editor,

I am writing with regard to the article featured in last Friday's paper. I do not agree with Sara Thornton's opinion; from my point of view she is wrong. It is not sugary food which makes our children obese and unhealthy but their lifestyle. While having nothing against modern technology, I do think that children spend far too long on their computers and too little time out in the fresh air. This is not just due to our cold and damp climate, but also to the media's attempts to create a climate of fear which results in parents being too frightened to allow their children to play outside.

Get writing

1

Sample answer:

Dear Itsuki,

I am writing to thank you for your hospitality during my recent stay in Shinshiro. I had a truly wonderful time and will never forget your generosity and kindness.

I am enclosing some photographs of my stay and I hope you will also enjoy the Italian *biscotti*. This is our very own traditional biscuit which we like to eat with coffee.

Please give my warmest wishes to your wife and children. Once again, thank you for your kindness. Should you ever find yourself in Milan please do not hesitate to get in touch.

Yours sincerely,

Francesca Pia

2

Sample answer:

Dear Mrs Martin,

I am writing to thank you for the wonderful stay my husband and I enjoyed at your hotel last month. Carcassonne is a beautiful city, but it was your friendly welcome and comfortable accommodation which made our trip so memorable. We enjoyed every moment of our stay and have recommended your hotel to all our friends.

I enclose a postcard of Ljubljana for your collection. My husband and I live about three kilometres away from this park.

Once again, many thanks for your kindness and hospitality.

Yours sincerely,

Karmen Veronik

3

Sample answer:

Dear Mayor MacManus,

I am writing with regard to the growing problem of litter in our city. As an environmental planner and parent of three young children, I feel that this problem not only spoils the look of our streets, but also poses a serious health risk to residents and wildlife.

Despite the considerable amount of money which has been spent on financing anti-litter campaigns, the problem has not improved. What needs to be worked on is increasing the number of bins in the city. The proprietors of fast food outlets should be spoken to regarding the amount of plastic packaging they distribute. A large percentage of the litter on our streets is generated by fast food wrappers and boxes.

I would like to request that this issue be addressed in your infrastructure programme. Your prompt attention to this matter would be greatly appreciated.

Yours sincerely,

Colin Lannigan

Unit 3   Writing online (1)

Looking closely

1

b

2

It is quite informal.

Language focus

1

1	b	2	c	3	d	4	a

2

These words make the sentences seem a little less bossy and a little more polite.

3

1	seems to be	3	couldn't
2	somewhat	4	may well

4

Sample answers:

1   It seems a little pointless going to Australia for four weeks. I would suggest either spending more time there or missing it out altogether.

2 Volunteer tourism does appear to be quite controversial. Many people suggest it possibly does more harm than good. I would do some research before agreeing to volunteer.

3 If you've already been to Brazil, you could always go somewhere new instead. It seems silly to spend all of your money on doing the same thing twice, don't you think?

Looking closely

1

c

2

The proposed bill calls for dogs to be kept on a lead in the park. This is because many people do not like dogs jumping up (and barking) at them and their children.

Language focus

1

This forum is generally more formal than the travel forum. Formal words and phrases include: *aware, enforce, penalised, vigilant, if you will, canine intimidation, distressing.*

2

1 As a responsible parent who is sick and tired of dogs running up and barking, sniffing, chasing and trying to bite my two year old, …

2 I'm very sorry to hear that dogs are constantly trying to bite your two year old. That must be very distressing for you and your child and I sympathize with you. Dog attacks are, however, very rare …

3 I got bitten by a dog at Inverboyne Park a few months ago, thanks to a dog owner being unable to control the excited animal.

4 Well, who are the responsible dog owners exactly? / What on earth is wrong with the odd dog-free park?

Get writing

1

Sample answers:

1

Hey everyone,

I'm planning my first ever trip to Brazil! I've never been before and would love some words of wisdom from all you experienced globetrotters out there. Any tips on where to go and what to see?

Thanks in advance!

2

My fiancé and I are getting married next year. We'd love a special day with all our friends and families. If anyone has any advice on how to plan a low-key budget wedding (we're both still students) then I would love to hear from you. Thanks!

2

Sample answers:

1

I know how you feel. I sometimes babysit my nephew in the holidays and it can be so hard especially when the weather is bad.

Has he got any friends from school who live nearby? Kids tend to be much happier and easier to deal with when they are with people their own age. You could also look at planning a trip into your nearest town one day – that might help him to expend some energy! Hope that helps you!

2

As someone who has been learning English for many years now, I feel for you. It's really difficult when you no longer have the option to go to classes. I sympathize! However, there does seem to be a lot of really good self-study material on the market – I would suggest investing in a couple of books and also possibly taking time to watch films, listen to music and read books in English – studying all the time can be somewhat tedious! All the best with your studies.

Unit 4   Writing online (2)

Looking closely

1

c

Language focus

1

1	Suva Crew	3	Suva Crew
2	Rocket Surgeon	4	Jennifer Owens and Suva Crew

2

Sample answer:

I'm not sure if I could function without my own portable window on the world. In the space of a few hours, I've used mine to read an important business document, check the weather in Shanghai (I'm heading there tomorrow and need to know what to pack) and answer a very important question from my three-year-old son (Mummy, what do snow tigers eat?). Do we really want to go back to the dark ages of TV weather forecasts, dusty encyclopaedias and snail mail?

3

1 b   2 a   3 d   4 c

Looking closely

1

b

2

Students' own answers.

Language focus

1

1 c   2 a   3 b

2

1 While   2 However
3 Admittedly / Yet

3

Sample answer:

While tourism is certainly beneficial for the economy in these times of financial insecurity, we cannot deny the grievous effects it has on the environment. However, halting the tourism industry completely would surely be counter-productive.

Get writing

1

Sample answer:

While many of the criticisms that you levy against smartphones are fair, I feel that we cannot ignore the advantages which technology gives the younger generation. Admittedly, the rise of cyber bullying has in all likelihood been brought about by the smartphone's ubiquity in teenage circles. However, as a teacher and mother, I think that smartphones also benefit young people, e.g. many teenagers learn a lot from educational apps.

2

Sample answer:

Thanks for this interesting post, Monica. I must say it sounds like you were a bit unlucky! While it's true that we will never win any prizes for good weather, we do often have sunny days in the summer! And yes, while there's no denying that some of our restaurants don't match up to Mediterranean ones, I think you would have been pleasantly surprised had you enjoyed a plate of our finest fish and chips. We do have a beautiful city: don't let one wet and unfortunate day put you off a return visit!

Unit 5   Planning

Looking closely

1

1   Dr Rae was Isobel's university tutor.

2   She is applying for a place on a postgraduate teaching course. Dr Rae mentions this and also refers to her teaching experience to date.

Language focus

1

1   states her position and how she knows Isobel

2   describes Isobel's personal and academic qualities

3   gives concrete, relevant examples of Isobel's abilities

4   ends on a positive note and offers to be of further assistance if necessary

2

1 e   2 b   3 c   4 d   5 a

3

1   She graduated in the top 5% of her class, a result which reflected her remarkably consistent standard of work: nearly half of her grades were the best in the class and most of the remainder were top 10%.

2   a confident, thoughtful and cheerful personality which made her a most welcome member of any tutorial

3   She is a most conscientious and motivated student, highly organized and utterly reliable.

4   Isobel has great experience of teaching. My department employed her in her final year as one of the five tutors on our access course / Isobel was also accepted onto the JET scheme for teaching English in Japan.

5   I taught Isobel on a number of occasions during her Masters degree in English at Appalachian State University.

4

conscientious, motivated, organized, reliable, confident, thoughtful, cheerful

5

Sample answers:

1   mature, caring, thoughtful, resourceful (You need to be mature when looking after children, as it is a very responsible task. You need to think about the needs of the children and care for them. It is important to be resourceful, as children need a lot of entertainment.)

2 conscientious, focused, articulate, dedicated
   (You need to work hard to succeed at university,
   and due to the volume of work you also need
   to be focused on getting your qualification, and
   achieving the tasks you have been set. You must
   be dedicated to see your course through, and your
   course might involve discussion and debate so you
   need to be able to articulate your ideas.)

3 creative, dynamic, innovative, competitive (This is
   a job which requires creative and fresh ideas. You
   need to be able to present your ideas in exciting
   ways and stay one step ahead of the competition.)

Looking closely

1

1 The first letter omits to mention how the writer
   knows Sergio. It does not support Sergio's
   personal qualities with any concrete evidence. The
   second reference does not give any information
   about Vanessa's specific achievements.

2 The first letter draws attention to a potentially
   negative feature, by referring to Sergio as 'a little
   dishevelled'. The second letter mentions Vanessa's
   political affiliation.

2

Sample answers:

1 I have known Sergio for three years. During
   this time he has regularly looked after my three
   children (all of whom are under the age of ten),
   often for extended periods of time.

2 Sergio has often impressed me with his ability to
   think on his feet. He once rescued my youngest
   daughter when a gust of wind had blown her into
   the sea. His quick decision to jump in after her and
   his excellent application of first aid skills saved her
   life.

3 During her time in this department, Vanessa
   organized a number of social initiatives which were
   greatly appreciated by the rest of the staff. She also
   won *The Northman's* Employee of the Year award
   on two occasions.

Language focus

1

b c a

2

Julia's outstanding interpersonal skills won her the
Summer Tours medal for customer service last year. In
addition to this, Julia was also frequently mentioned
by name in positive feedback provided by our own
customer surveys. Part of Julia's success in working with
tourists comes from her natural flair with languages,
and she has proven her commitment to further
improving her linguistic skills through her decision to
study for a degree in modern languages.

Get writing

1

Sample answer:

Dear Mrs Jackson,

Xiaoloi Li has worked as a part-time waitress in Latte
Paradiso for eighteen months. I have been Xiaoloi's
line manager during this time and I have formed a very
favourable impression of her skills and abilities.

Xialoi is a reliable and resourceful worker, whose kind
and helpful personality has been appreciated by all the
staff and customers at Latte Paradiso. She is an efficient
and enthusiastic waitress who takes her work very
seriously.

Foreign visitors have often complimented Xiaoloi on
her ability to converse in different languages. I am
sure, therefore, that she will be an asset to the tourist
office.

I am more than happy to vouch for Xiaoloi's honesty
and efficiency; she would be an asset to any workplace.
Should you require any further information please do
not hesitate to contact me.

Yours sincerely,

Philip Grabe

2

Sample answer:

Dear Dr Roth,

I have taught Matt Donnell biology for two years,
and in this time I have been most impressed by his
commitment and dedication to his studies.

Matt has consistently achieved A grades in biology this
year, and has often supported students less able than
himself. He performs very well in group work and his
classmates have all appreciated his gentle sense of
humour and kind nature.

I was delighted to award Matt with the biology prize
this year. His hard work and effort have truly earned
him it, and his dissertation on cardiovascular disease
would have been a credit to any undergraduate
student.

There is little doubt in my mind that Matt will make an
outstanding nurse. I commend him to you.

Yours sincerely,

Joyce Hogan

3

Sample answer:

Dear Mr Khan,

Francesca Contari has worked as a PA in our accounts
department for five years. During this time she has
performed a wide range of administrative tasks to a
very high standard.

Francesca is highly motivated and organized. Her
dynamic, enthusiastic nature has made her very

popular in our department. Francesca can always be relied upon and has a wonderful eye for detail. I will be very sorry to lose her, but I am sure that her unflagging energy will be of great service to her and others in the work she is hoping to do.

Francesca's excellent work recently earned her a promotion. I feel that her decision to forgo this

and work as a volunteer speaks volumes about her generous and determined personality.

I support Francesca's application wholeheartedly. Should you have any further questions, please do not hesitate to contact me.

Yours sincerely,

Alice Mills

Unit 6   Structuring

Looking closely

1

1   Klaus is applying for the post of intern journalist.
2   someone with experience of writing, good time management skills, ability to meet deadlines, adaptability and resourcefulness

Language focus

1

1   d, g   2   b, h   3   e, f   4   a, c

2

writing, discovering, admired, welcome, hone, illustrates, plays, contributed, maintain, won, combining, developed, organizing, believe, possess, learned, participated, relish, relocating, look forward to. The verbs are active.

3

1 a   2 b   3 a   4 a

They sound better because they use active verbs. This makes it sound as if the writer played an active part in their achievement. An overreliance on the passive voice is not a good thing in covering letters, as it can make the writer look 'acted upon' rather than active.

4

1   It has been my dream to become a newspaper journalist since I was at high school.
2   Working in five different retail environments in the past few years has allowed me to learn new skills in each one.
3   Whilst the power of qualifications is unarguable, I also believe that those who work hard will be rewarded for their efforts.
4   Despite the fact that my time working in an office has been fairly minimal to date, the experiences I have had have been varied and extremely useful.

Looking closely

1

No, neither of these covering letters would be taken seriously.

Language focus

1

1   Text A and Text B. Text B sounds particularly egocentric, as every sentence begins with *I*.
2   Text A. It mentions that the writer has never had any work published.
3   Text A. It is not relevant that the writers' friends and uncle think the writer should be a writer.
4   Text A and Text B. Text B lists a lot of adjectives, but makes no attempt to back these up with evidence.
5   Text B. (*being employed by your company, your online magazine has always appealed to me, my work has been published*)

2

Sample answer:

I am really interested in working for your company, as I find your online magazine extremely well written and interesting. Writing has always played an important role in my life, and I regularly contribute to online travel sites and the local newspaper.

My academic record is extremely strong, and I have managed to combine my studies with a range of other interests. Editing the school magazine required a lot of hard work, creativity and focus.

Get writing

1

Students' own answers.

2

Sample answer:

1

Dear Mr Black,

I am writing in response to the advertisement for sales director which I found on the Sales Europa website last week. I am currently Sales Manager for PC Planet Ltd, where I have expanded sales by more than 75 per cent annually since taking up my position three years ago.

As you can see from my CV, I have consistently increased sales in each of the companies I have worked with to date. In addition to this, I have managed to develop new business opportunities on an international level. It was under my leadership that PC Planet broke into the Scandinavian and Middle Eastern markets.

As International Sales Director for your company, I would aim to expand your business opportunities and increase profitability, building on my experience and contacts.

In addition to my achievements in sales over the past five years, I have focused on developing my academic qualifications and have recently graduated with a Masters in Marketing and Sales Management.

I would be happy to answer any questions you may have at interview. I look forward to hearing from you.

Yours sincerely,

Silke Wessel

2

Dear Ms Bennett,

I am writing to apply for the position of Overseas Representative which I saw advertised on the Work Europe website last week. I am currently in my final year of studying for a degree in modern languages, and I would welcome the opportunity this position would give me to practise my Italian.

As my CV demonstrates, I have proven experience of working in the hospitality industry and also of leading a team. Last summer I worked for a holiday camp in the UK where I was responsible for a team of five employees. My daily duties focused on ensuring the comfort and well-being of holidaymakers and motivating my team of workers. I hold a full driving licence.

I look forward to hearing from you.

Yours sincerely,

Kate Black

Unit 7   Developing

Looking closely

1

b

Language focus

1

1	Paragraph 1	3	Paragraph 4
2	Paragraph 2	4	Paragraph 3

2

mom, good mother, child-rearing, mothers, kids, children, generations, parents, parenting, kid
soccer-watchers, snack-selectors, flashcard-flashers, all-seven-volumes-of-Harry-Potter readers, college-essay editors, Candyland rivals, parents, generations
intensive parenting, helicoptered kids, sadder, fatter, less resilient, play less actively, directing, negative emotion, cosseted, give up, over-controlling, depression, less satisfaction

3

1 d   2 e   3 b   4 c   5 a
Students' own answers.

4

1 c   2 a   3 b
Students' own answers.

5

1	obsessed	3	tender	5	idolize
2	airbrushed	4	glitterati	6	self-esteem

Looking closely

1

the generation of adults who refuse to grow up

2

personal experience

Language focus

1

a, b, e

2

These are topic sentences. Each sentence introduces and states a new layer of the writer's argument. The rest of the paragraph then adds weight to the idea expressed in the topic sentence through examples, illustrations and evidence.

Get writing

Sample answer:

Teenagers do not leave home early enough.

Living with your parents until you are well into your thirties is commonplace nowadays. In households all over the country, fully-grown men and women are raiding the fridge and enjoying the luxury of a personal door-to-(bedroom) door laundry and ironing service. Blame the job situation, blame the economic climate, blame the housing shortage. But by letting our teenagers mooch around the family home, we are not doing them any favours.

Of my university friends, a good fifty per cent boomeranged back to Mum and Dad after graduation and are still there now. These friends hold down good jobs, they dress well and enjoy good social lives. So why haven't they embraced that old rite of passage – getting your very own place and living alone?

My friend Bob is unashamedly pragmatic about his decision to live with his parents. 'Yeah, it's not like I don't have the money', he says. 'But I've had my day of living in flats and arguing over whose turn it is to take the bins out. At least I know the food in the fridge is fresh and that I'll get my dinner every

evening.' My school friend Rachel still lives in the family home, although she is planning to leave when she gets married. 'Living with mum and dad helps me to save the money I need', she says.

One thing's for sure – the boomerang children are not moving anywhere fast. What will happen when these boomerang children (dependent, lazy, cosseted) raise their own children? Now that's a sight I'm not looking forward to.

Unit 8   Being clear

Looking closely

1

1   how to make a fig cake
2   Yes, they are very clear. No extra information is included in the main body of the instructions. She has listed everything that Stanya will need to complete the task, and she has described what will happen if Stanya follows the instructions correctly. Katie has also numbered the steps, so the order is very clear.

Language focus

1

1	recipe	3	recipe	5	recipe
2	note	4	note	6	recipe

2

1 b   2 e   3 a   4 c   5 d

3

Sample answer:

Pull the carrot tops off the carrots.

Add the butter. Then sift the flour. Next, grease the cake tin.

Add the eggs one at a time.

Garnish the top with finely chopped parsley.

Add hot chillies if you want.

4

some soap (how much?), *button* (which?), *the other button* (which?), *twiddle* (*imprecise*) takes ages (how long?)

Sample answer:

Put one laundry tablet into the small drawer on the top left-hand corner of the machine.

Turn the button directly below the red button clockwise to select the temperature.

Push the large red button on the right-hand side of the machine.

The cycle takes about two hours and is quite noisy!

5

1 c 2 b 3 d 4 a 5 e Adding these sentences lets the reader know what to expect at the different stages in the procedure.

Looking closely

1

These instructions are a bit wordy at times, which makes them not as clear to follow as they could be.

2

Considering that these instructions are written for a friend the language is very cold and formal. The writer has used the passive voice on more than one occasion.

Language focus

1

These sentences use the passive voice: *The children should be bathed. They should be given toys to play with. Make sure they aren't given anything which will get ruined. The children should be taken out of the bath before they begin to squabble.*

2

No. It is more suitable for formal, impersonal instructions.

3

1   They should be given toys to play with.
2   Read them a story.
3   Let the children watch TV while you run a bath.

Get writing

1

Sample answer:

Top 20 log

20 digestive biscuits

20 glace cherries

20 marshmallows

a tin of condensed milk

coconut flakes

First crush the digestive biscuits.

Chop the marshmallows and glace cherries.

Stir the marshmallows and cherries into the biscuit crumbs.

Stir a tin of condensed milk into the mixture. It will get very sticky.

Take the mixture out of the bowl and roll it into a log shape.

Sprinkle with coconut flakes and put in the fridge to chill for two hours.

2

Sample answer:

First, switch the cooker on at the wall. A red light should come on when you've done this. Turn the knobs along the front of the cooker clockwise if you want to use the hob. The button to the left of the clock controls the top oven. Turn the button to the right of the clock to use the fan oven.

Switch the washing machine on at the wall. Put two laundry tablets in the left hand side of the drawer. Turn the large white button clockwise to choose the right temperature. The cycle takes about two and a half hours – be warned!

Unit 9   Being precise and factual

Looking closely

1

1   Laura wants to make a travel insurance claim after a flood damaged her possessions when she was on holiday.

2   No. This report does not describe her feelings.

3   The tone is neutral. The language is formal and objective. Laura recounts the facts in a precise way. She does not describe her feelings, or include any irrelevant information.

Language focus

1

1   the overflow pipe in the apartment where I was staying became disconnected from the storage tank

2   On the morning of Tuesday 15 October / that afternoon

3   I have kept the damaged goods for your inspection.

4   Puerto Pollensa, Majorca / the apartment where I was staying

2

The report includes irrelevant information (*a perfect day on the beach*), it describes his feelings (*I was so happy!*), and it is vague (*one day on my holiday, my things*).

3

At around 3 p.m. on 14 June (the second day of my holiday in Gouves, Crete) I returned from the beach to find that a fire had destroyed the Andreas apartment building where I was staying. The fire was caused by old and faulty wiring. My luggage, including my clothes and camera, was destroyed.

4

On the afternoon of Wednesday 3 August I was sitting at Stand 3 of Victoria Bus Station, London, where I was waiting for the 15:35 bus to Glasgow. At around 15:15 I asked a man to watch my backpack while I bought some juice at the coach station café. The man was in his thirties with short, brown hair. He was wearing a red anorak. He agreed to watch my backpack. When I returned, the backpack and the man had disappeared. The backpack contained my clothes, make-up and mp3 player.

5

1   It is not clear how fast the car was going and how exactly it lost control.

2   It is not clear how much money was lost or what the important stuff was.

3   It is not clear who was finding it difficult to walk.

4   It is not clear exactly when the accident happened.

6

1   The car, which looked like it was driving at about 100 km per hour, skidded onto the other side of the road.

2   My wallet, which contained 50 euros in cash and my credit card, was stolen.

3   We suspect the man, who was finding it difficult to walk, was drunk.

4   On the afternoon of 1 February I broke my leg when skiing in the Tatra mountains.

7

It would sound as if Laura had more than one suitcase with her.

8

1   Non-defining relative clause. Commas should be added.

2   This could be a defining or non-defining relative clause depending on how many daughters the speaker has.

3   Non-defining relative clause. Commas should be added. The exception would be if there were some firefighters who arrived slowly.

4   Defining relative clause.

9

1   We use *who* for people: My friend who came with me on holiday was also injured in the crash.

2   This should be a non-defining relative clause and needs commas: My passport, which goes everywhere with me, was in the small leather bag.

3   We do not use *what* to introduce relative clauses: We stayed in the whitewashed hotel which has windows overlooking the sea.

4   We do not repeat the subject after a relative clause: A teacher who is also qualified in first aid helped me stop my nosebleed.

5   A relative clause needs to follow the noun to which it refers: The thief, who was wearing a leather jacket, jumped into a white sports car.

6   We need *two* commas to separate non-defining relative clauses: My expensive hairdryer, which my husband gave me only last month, exploded last night.

10

Dear Mr Peters,

On 15th December 2013 I was injured in an automobile accident with your insured, Angela Rogers. I was heading towards Lee River when I slowed down at some roadworks ~~what~~ which were placed at the entrance of the bridge.

As I slowed down, your insured ~~rammed~~ drove into the back of my car. The force of the impact ~~hurled~~ pushed me forwards and I felt a snapping sensation in my neck. Later that night I woke with a splitting headache ~~who~~ which did not respond to painkillers. The pain gradually travelled down my neck and into my back. As a result of this injury, I was forced to miss many Christmas family gatherings over the festive period. ~~My wife who is usually patient says I've been a misery to live with!~~

On top of the pain I have experienced, I have had to miss three weeks of building work, resulting in an estimated loss of earnings of £1,500. My back, which still constantly feels quite painful, is particularly sore when I lift heavy objects. ~~This is hardly ideal for someone in my line of work.~~

As a result of this injury and my consequent considerable loss of earnings, I would like to be compensated £2,500.

I look forward to hearing from you at your earliest convenience.

Yours faithfully,
Kelvin Briggs

Get writing

1

Sample answer:

Dear Sir,

Policy number: BEL 790 321

I am writing to make a claim on the above insurance policy to compensate for medical expenses I incurred during my skiing holiday in Slovakia.

On the afternoon of Wednesday 29 January I broke my leg after a collision with a fellow skier.

My leg needed urgent medical attention and on my doctor's advice I spent two days in hospital. After being discharged from hospital, I returned to Spain on the morning of 1 February.

Please find attached the contact details of the hospital where I was treated and scanned copies of my medical bill and additional airline charges.

I look forward to hearing from you,

Yours faithfully,
Carola Cabana

2

Sample answer:

At around 13:30 on Thursday 3 September, Julia Ferrier and I were standing by the photocopier waiting to collect some documents. Julia collected her papers, and as she turned to go, the belt on her jacket got caught on the photocopier. She turned around, and the sudden movement pulled the machine off the table and onto her foot. Brian Nugent and I lifted the photocopier off her foot and carried Julia to a seat in the reception area. Julia seemed to be in a considerable amount of pain, and Brian called an ambulance immediately. While we waited, I applied an ice compress to her foot, but it seemed to do little to relieve her pain. The ambulance arrived five minutes later and Julia was taken to hospital.

Unit 10 Improving

Looking closely

1

In Text A, the intended reader is a prospective employer. In Text B, the intended readers are contributors to an online discussion forum so anyone could read the post.

2

Text A: the writer has not structured the covering letter well, e.g. there are no paragraphs. The writer has also used inappropriately informal register, e.g. *ad, top, get along very well*. The expression *long range of customers* is incorrect – it should say *wide range of customers*. He has not signed off properly.

Text B: the writer needs to use paragraphs, and rethink their choice of words, e.g. *lot to be desire, a new breath of wind, don't have where to shop, heighten employment, cheap and fashion items*. The writer has also repeated the phrase *I don't agree with you* in two consecutive sentences.

Language focus

1

3, 4, 9, 10

2

the lack of paragraphing

3

Text A

Dear Mrs Giles,

I came across your advertisement for the post of receptionist online and am writing to attach my CV.

I have worked in the customer service industry for ten years and have experience of working with an extremely wide range of customers. I believe I have the stamina, attention to detail and enthusiasm which the position requires.

My hobbies include travel. I speak fluent French and German and this has always enabled me to communicate effectively with clients.

Many thanks for your time in reading this email. I look forward to hearing from you.

Yours sincerely,

Sam

Text B

Hi Keiko, I'm sorry but I don't agree with you at all.

The building of a new store will be very beneficial to our town. For a long time now people have been forced to shop at overpriced small businesses where the customer service can sometimes leave a lot to be desired.

This new store will bring a breath of fresh air into our community. It will also increase employment, and will give people new pride in their town. Why would we want to live in the past anyway?

For many years now people have been complaining that they don't have anywhere to shop for cheap and fashionable items. Now they can find what they want.

4

Text A could contain more information about the writer's skills. The writer of Text B should omit repetitive language, e.g. *I do not agree with you.*

5

The sentences all begin with *I* which sounds egotistical. The writer should vary the way the sentences begin, e.g. changing *I have worked in the customer service industry* to *Having had the experience of working with ...*

6

1   •   The writer has not used paragraphs to structure her ideas.

      •   She has included unnecessary information about Katrin's personal life.

      •   The writer could also perhaps provide a little more detail about Katrin's academic performance.

2

Sample answer:

I have been Katrin's English teacher for five years. Throughout this time, she has always impressed me with her punctuality, creativity and positive attitude.

She has also performed consistently well in classroom assignments, working equally well in both group and individual tasks. Katrin also won the Student of the Year award at our school's prize-giving ceremony last summer in recognition of her excellent attendance and results.

I cannot recommend Katrin's work highly enough: she would be an asset to any organisation.

Looking closely

1

A   a reference letter

B   a formal letter of complaint

C   a semi-formal email

D   a blog comment

E   an extract from an opinion piece or blog

Language focus

1

1 B   2 C   3 A   4 E   5 D

2

1 Vlad is highly motivated and organized. His dynamic, enthusiastic nature has made him very popular in our department. Vlad can always be relied upon to produce his best work and has a wonderful eye for detail. I will be very sorry to lose him, but I am sure that his unflagging energy will be of great service to him and others in the work he is hoping to do.

2 I am writing with regard to the high levels of noise in my neighbourhood between the hours of ten o'clock in the evening and two o'clock in the morning. While I am aware that us city dwellers cannot expect complete tranquillity, I genuinely believe that the constant levels of noise and disturbance in the street outside our house are having a negative impact on my family's health.

3 You asked me about the location of our flat. We live in the Saint Denis area of Paris, within easy walking distance of some wonderful shops and cafés. There's a tram stop right outside our house, so you can travel around the city very easily. I see from your Flat Swap profile that you are interested in history – are you planning to visit any of our world famous museums?

4 Thank you for writing this really interesting post. As a language student myself, I empathize with your account of the trials and tribulations of learning English!

5 In this age of high unemployment and severe financial hardship it is understandable that such a high number of people choose to seek their fortune abroad.

Get writing

Students' own answers.

Unit 11   Showing disappointment

Looking closely

1

He complains about the accommodation and the activity programme.

2

Yes. Jovan records his experiences in a logical and sequenced order. He appeals to the reader's sympathy by mentioning on more than one occasion how much he had been looking forward to the trip and how hard he had been saving for it. His account is balanced (he mentions the positive aspects of the summer school too) and although he is clearly upset, his writing remains polite at all times.

Language focus

1

disappointed

2

deep disappointment, I had been thoroughly looking forward to, I am afraid, failed to live up to my expectations, less than picturesque, I had been eagerly anticipating, I was dumped, a long awaited, once in a life time trip, cost me over two years' hard work and saving.

3

"in the heart of Edinburgh" is a direct quote from the brochure. It provides evidence of what Jovan was promised.

"guide" is also a direct quote from the brochure. The fact that Jovan uses inverted commas shows that he does not feel that it is really correct to describe this person in such a way. It is an ironic device, which Jovan gets away with using as the rest of his email is very polite.

"check things out" – the guide's remark was quite dismissive, so Jovan does well to show that this is what she actually said. This direct quote emphasizes how offhand she was.

4

to make him feel ashamed of himself, to make him feel sorry for Jovan, to make him rethink his staff recruitment and training procedures

Looking closely

1

The tone of this extract is humorous. The writer is trying to make his points through making jokes and using sarcasm, but it is unlikely that this will have the desired effect. His insults about Scottish cooking might upset the reader. His writing is too informal, and as a result, his complaint will not be taken seriously.

2

you Scots don't exactly have a reputation for great cooking / these wonderfully exciting and informative cultural tours you'd laid on for us (not!).

Language focus

1

1 *Afraid* sounds polite. *Sorry* sounds too apologetic.

2 *Readily* indicates Jovan's surprise that the guide was happy to admit that she had no knowledge of Edinburgh. *Grudgingly* suggests an awareness that she should have at least visited the city before.

3 *Dumped* is emotive. It conveys the lack of respect with which Jovan feels he was treated. *Dropped off* is much more neutral.

4 *Over two years' hard work and saving* is more emotive than *just over £3000 in total* as it emphasizes the effort Jovan put in to paying for his trip.

5 *Would like* to be is polite and measured. *Insist on being* is much more combative.

2

1 very disappointing
2 delighted
3 fell far short of my expectations
4 seriously undercooked
5 experiencing a busy night
6 somewhat distracted
7 less than relaxing evening
8 appreciate your reassurance

Get writing

1

Sample answer:

On my first day of wearing these shoes the heel came apart from the sole. Quite apart from the fact that this could have been dangerous, I was in an interview at the time. I'm sure you can appreciate how embarrassed and upset I felt when this happened in front of the entire interview panel. This certainly does not match up to previous experiences I have had of the excellent quality of your shoes.

2

Sample answers:

1 Dear Mrs Hall,

I have just returned from a holiday in the Pyrénées at your Mountain Retreat cottages. Your brochure mentions "clear air, tranquillity and a welcome escape from the hustle and bustle of city life". Well, as my family and I live in a busy city, this is exactly what we were looking for.

However, I am sorry to say we did not get the peace we so craved. Our "mountain retreat" was, in fact, located right next to a building site. We had to leave the cottage at eight o'clock every morning before the building work started. My wife, who is currently recovering from major surgery, had a splitting headache from the incessant thumping and banging which we were subjected to at all hours. I did not feel it was safe for my children to play in the garden, as the builders appeared to be using it as a storage area for building equipment. My son has severe asthma, and the large dust clouds which were constantly being created by the building work did nothing to help his condition.

Despite these inconveniences, our concierge went out of her way to help. Her numerous acts of kindness (which included driving my wife to hospital in the middle of the night) did not go unappreciated. However, I feel that we deserve some explanation for the discrepancies between what is described in your brochure and the reality of a holiday at Mountain Retreats. My family and I would like a full refund for the cost of this accommodation, and look forward to hearing from you at your earliest convenience.

Yours sincerely,

Istvan Magyar

2 Dear Jacques,

I've always been a fan of your great dishes, culinary flair and the cosy ambience of your restaurant. However, my last few dining experiences have not been up to scratch. The members of staff you have recently recruited just don't offer the friendly welcome I've come to expect.

The last few times I've turned up and asked for a table my "hello" has been rewarded with a sullen stare. The menu has been unceremoniously tossed in my direction rather than handed to me with a smile. Last night I waited for half an hour before one of your waiting staff decided to take my order. There was no apology or acknowledgement of my wait.

Jacques, your restaurant has been the best in town until now, and I hope I can keep on eating at yours for a long time to come. Could you let me know what you intend to do about this situation?

With many thanks and very best wishes,

Rik Gallante

Unit 12   Being polite but firm

Looking closely

1

1 They are friends. Malu has recently stayed at Klara's holiday cottage.

2 Klara asks Malu to let her know when accidents happen and to repair and replace broken items.

2

Klara's email is really polite and friendly. However, she makes it clear that she is disappointed about the mess in her cottage. Malu will probably feel really ashamed when she reads it. She might offer to pay for the damages, and it is likely that she will apologize.

Language focus

1

1 I was also wondering if you might be able to shed some light on what has happened to the white living room rug.

2 Hope you're well and enjoying this fine summer weather. Plenty of good opportunities for surfing where you are, I should think!

3 Being a bit of a butterfingers myself, I know only too well that these things happen. Heinz doesn't call me Calamity Klara for nothing!

4 it would be great if you could let me know when accidents happen and replace or repair broken items

5 It was great to hear about your new job by the way. I knew that red jacket would go down well at interview!

6 casualties in the crockery department

2

1 Indirect questions are more polite and less combative than direct questions.

2 This opening comment sets a friendly tone – it reassures Malu that Klara does not want to jeopardize their friendship.

3 The self-deprecating remark is humorous – it directs the focus away from Malu's wrongdoings (by focusing on Klara's own clumsiness) and lightens the overall mood.

4 This request makes it clear that although Klara wants to remain friends with Malu, she also wants action to be taken.

5 This remark ends the email on a positive note, and reinforces the friendliness at the beginning of the letter.

6 This euphemism is a gentler way of saying 'you have smashed all my dishes' or something similar.

3

what has happened to the white living room rug / it has been totally ruined

4

Sample answer:

I was a bit surprised to find you have totally ruined it – are these coffee stains? This sentence sounds much more accusatory. It also leaves no room for the (very slim) possibility that it might not have been Malu who ruined the carpet.

5

1 d   2 a   3 b   4 c

Looking closely

1

Alex has delivered training sessions at Ms Tallis' business.

Language focus

1

It politely states the situation and asks for action to be taken. However, it is much more business like and less friendly than Klara's email.

2

Alex does not use humour. This is a business email, and he feels that the late payment is too serious a matter to joke about.

3

Human subject: I'm just writing to check …, I completed the work three months ago, I run a small-scale business …

Impersonal subject: The amount has not yet been transferred into my account …, … the invoice has been processed …

Using a human subject (I) underlines the fact that Alex is a person, who is suffering upset and inconvenience. The impersonal subject shifts the blame away from Ms Tallis and suggests that it may be larger, more impersonal forces which have caused the delay in payment. Alex therefore increases the reader's sympathy for his situation, while avoiding a combative, accusatory tone.

4

1 I have yet to receive payment.

2 I haven't been able to get through to you.

3 This situation cannot be allowed to continue.

4 Should you be experiencing difficulties making this payment, please contact me so that we can discuss a possible solution.

5 I take pride in my work, and am very disappointed at the long delay I have experienced in receiving payment.

Get writing

1

Sample answer:

No. His email is not firm enough.

Hello Tadas,

How are things with you? Fernando tells me you're going to his birthday weekend in Berlin – looks like it'll be a fun weekend!

I'm also really keen to come to Berlin if finances allow … Talking of which, I was wondering if you could pay me back that hundred pounds I lent you two months ago? Like you, I'm saving to start uni – I'm sure you understand how every penny counts right now. I've attached my bank details so you can just bung it into my account. Do you think you'd be able to pay it in by next week so I can book my train tickets?

See you on that train to Berlin, hopefully!

Cheers,

Andris

2

Sample answer:

Dear Rosita,

I've been missing your thoughtful and cheerful presence in my English classes, and I do hope that everything is alright with you. I'm really sorry to have to remind you about the college policy: if your absence continues I will have no choice but to withhold your class certificate. It would be a terrible shame to have to forfeit your place on the course. Also, I have not yet received your last three essays – I was wondering how you are getting on with these?

Should you wish to discuss this, please do not hesitate to contact me. I really hope we can come to a solution which will enable you to continue your studies here.

Kind regards,

Dinara Antonovich

3

Sample answer:

Dear Nancy,

I hope this finds you well and that you enjoyed a restful weekend.

I am writing to enquire about whether a replacement has been found for Marilyn's post. A month has passed since she resigned, and I am finding my workload increasingly heavy. Not only do I continue to do all my own administrative duties, I find I have also been assigned Marilyn's jobs too. I know my alias is 'Wonderwoman', however I feel that filling two jobs is more than even a superhero like me can achieve.

Having worked 'til nine every night this week I am keen to resolve this matter as quickly as possible. I was wondering if we could perhaps meet to discuss this at a time which suits you.

Kind regards,

Vaila

4

Sample answer:

Dear Mr and Mrs Webster,

Hope this finds you well. I've tried to call you a few times but haven't managed to get through.

It's great to see Magnus in our club. He has a lot of enthusiasm for outdoor activities, which is marvellous to see. I was wondering, however, if you could perhaps have a word with Magnus about the club code (see attached). There have been a few complaints from the younger children about bullying behaviour and I would like to put a stop to this before it gets any more serious. If you could read and discuss the code with Magnus before next week I would be very grateful.

I do hope Magnus enjoys his time at the club. We're canoeing next week, so remind him to wrap up warm!

Best wishes,

Anne Marie Johnson

Unit 13   Remaining balanced

Looking closely

1

1   The texts are about the environmentally unsustainable sources which a major toy manufacturing company uses to produce its toys.

2   Both texts request that the toy manufacturer seeks an alternative source for its products.

3   Mr Howard is probably the company director.

2

Text B is more effective as it is written in a balanced, factual and polite tone. In contrast, Text A sounds hysterical. It is also offensive: *You make me sick*.

Language focus

1

1   It has recently come to my attention that Play Time's toys are manufactured using pulp and paper sourced from endangered rainforests.

2 The plight of these rainforest's endangered wildlife has been publicized recently in the international press and world media.

3 Furthermore, it is well known that you make great profits from the sale of your toys, while doing nothing at all to offset the environmental damage your actions result in.

4 This is unacceptable.

5 It is time for you to confront the serious consequences your industry is having on the environment, and find a more sustainable source for your products.

2

shocked, horrified, moved to tears of deep sorrow, fat cats, luxuriate, plundered, innocent, misery

3

1 d   2 c   3 e   4 b   5 a

4

1 biased   3 neutral   5 biased
2 biased   4 neutral

Looking closely

1

1 animals
2 very concerned
3 unacceptable
4 humane and ethical practice
5 address this very important matter

Language focus

1

1 your cosmetics company uses products which are tested on animals
2 I was very concerned to read about this in the national press
3 Many other leading cosmetic companies now test their beauty products dermatologically
4 Please confirm that you have taken steps to address this very important matter.

2

1 The new motorway will endanger local wildlife.
2 I would like to ask you to stop testing your beauty products on animals.
3 Global warming is gradually increasing the temperature of the earth and is likely to have detrimental effects on life on this planet.
4 If this school closes down, the students' education will be considerably disrupted.

Get writing

1

Sample answer:

Dear Mr Kertes,

I understand that plans are underway for a Price-rite to be built in Szentes. As someone who has lived and worked all my life in this town, I am very concerned about the effect that this new superstore will have on our local businesses and on the overall look of the town.

Szentes is often described as an "unspoilt haven" in tourist brochures, and it seems likely that people's perception of the town will change if plans to build a Price-rite go ahead. As the tourist industry generates a large percentage of the town's income, the decision to build this store is hard to understand.

I would be very grateful if you could confirm that a public vote will be held on this matter. I look forward to hearing from you.

Yours sincerely,

Katalin Pluhar

2

Sample answer:

Dear Mr Leslie,

It has come to my attention that workers often experience unsatisfactory working conditions on banana plantations, where they are poorly paid and inadequately housed. As a regular shopper at your store I want the fruit I buy to have been fairly traded.

I am asking you to confirm that you only buy bananas from suppliers who pay their farmers a fair wage.

Yours sincerely,

Yvonne Johnson

3

Sample answer:

Dear Ms Grierson,

I understand that many of the toys manufactured by Kinder-Time contain phthalates. As a father of two small children, I do not want to buy toys which contain these chemical compounds.

Recent studies have linked these chemicals to a range of different cancers and hormonal malfunctions and I do not think they should be included in any product made for children.

I would be grateful if you could confirm that Kinder-Time is taking steps to address this very important matter.

Yours sincerely,

David Riddell

Unit 14   Being light-hearted

Looking closely

1

1   to entertain her readers
2   She was too excited about getting out into the beautiful spring evening, and didn't want to hang around. She locked the door behind her (so Brett was left locked in the flat).
3   The neighbour couldn't see where the sound was coming from, and Brett was making a funny mistake as he can't speak Hungarian very well.

Language focus

1

1 b	3 f	5 e
2 d	4 c	6 a

2

has sprung, I'd been slaving, couldn't wait to get out, breathing in, listening to, sprinted, dumped, called, dashed, locked, wandered, was, have I mentioned, is jammed, we've been meaning, fixed, free, knelt, peered, decided, saw, happened, lives, mustered, called, was calling, looked, was offering, beat, returned, felt, had spent, have made, will stop, think, rush off, is learning

Tenses used: Present perfect (has sprung), Past perfect (had spent), Past Perfect continuous (I'd been slaving), Past simple (couldn't wait), Past continuous (was calling), Present simple (lives), Future simple (will stop), Present continuous (is learning).

3

1	been travelling	4	fell
2	had been wandering	5	left
3	was pulling out		

4

Sample answers:

1   Francisco decided to look for work in another country. He had lost his job and failed his exams, so he wanted to make a new start.
2   Marie and Daniel arrived at their hotel at midnight. They'd had a long and tiring journey and on their way had been robbed.
3   Ludovic couldn't believe it when his dinner guest said she was on a diet. He'd spent the whole day cooking and had baked an enormous rhubarb cake!
4   Mark went travelling around the world. He'd won a lot of money and he'd bought a camper van.

5

Julia takes a cliché, and adapts it slightly, e.g. *slaving over a hot oven* becomes *slaving over a hot photocopier.* She keeps the tone chatty and conversational by asking questions (*Have I mentioned that there is only one window in our flat and that it is jammed?*) making conversational asides (*We've been meaning to get it fixed for ages …*) and using humour wherever possible through her choice of words, e.g. *peered, slaved, blissful.*

6

1 c	2 a	3 b	4 e	5 d

7

slave: this verb conveys the excessively hard work Julia feels she has been doing.

stifling: this adjective stresses the extreme discomfort Brett would have felt as he was locked in the flat. *Hot* would have not conveyed his desperation so successfully.

peer: this is a more humorous verb than *look*. The reader can visualise Brett's intense concentration and this adds humour to the anecdote.

blissful: this emphasises the contrast between Julia's happiness and Brett's frustration, and again, adds humour.

stroll: this verb describes a pleasant relaxing walk. Again, it adds humour through its connotations of freedom and relaxation (a contrast with Brett's imprisonment). *Walk* does not convey the same sense of relaxation.

8

1	scoffed	4	hens	7	shuffled
2	dreaming	5	deserted		
3	gaggle	6	gaunt		

Look closely

1

3, 1, 2

2

The writer could have included a bit more information about how this experience affected her mood during the trip. Did it affect the relationship between her and their friend? Did they fall out? Perhaps the experience brought them closer together.

Get writing

1

Sample answer:

I had always wanted to try horse riding, so my travels in Mongolia seemed the perfect opportunity to realize this lifelong dream. I arrived at the riding school full of enthusiasm for learning a new skill – what I hadn't realized was that the teachers' average age was twelve years old and that their teaching seemed very much based on the 'sink or swim' school of teaching.

My teacher was an eleven year old with a shock of black hair and a wide, rather cheeky grin. He and his horse set off ahead of me at an elegant canter while I gripped the reins of my horse for dear life and wished the next hour of my life away. The horse, sensing my fear, whinnied, grumbled and twitched erratically as we galloped over the dusty plain.

By the time we had completed our circuit every bone in my body was aching and my knuckles had turned a funny shade of blue. I slid off my horse and stumbled away on legs like jelly. Next time I feel like seeing a country from a different perspective, I might just hire a bike!

2

Sample answer:

The night of my great aunt Nelly's sixtieth birthday was the most embarrassing night of my life. I'd just been promoted and was feeling flush, so I booked us a table at this very fancy new restaurant in town. You know the kind of place: six starters before you even get to the main course, more cutlery than you know what to do with – in a word, posh.

Well, Aunt Nelly was very impressed. She said it was great that I had finally made something of my life. I told her she could have whatever she wanted and she did. We both did: lobster, caviar, truffles – the works.

You can probably guess what's coming next. I went to pay the bill with a flourish – and my card was refused (it had expired the day before). Aunt Nelly had to foot the entire bill. Of course, I paid her back three days later, but she's never let me forget it!

3

Sample answer:

My memories of childhood are all a bit fuzzy, but I do have one very early memory which I remember quite clearly. I must have been about three and my mum had gone out into the garden to hang out some washing, leaving me alone in the house.

I was playing around with the key in the door. I suppose I must have accidentally locked my Mum out, because the next thing I remember is her flushed face looming crossly behind the glass pane in the door. She was gesticulating wildly, and I remember feeling panicky as I realized that what I had done might not be so easy to undo …

I must have managed to unlock the door in the end. My Mum clearly wasn't as traumatized by this incident as I was – whenever I've mentioned it she says she doesn't remember it at all!

Unit 15 Creating mood

Looking closely

1

1   two
2   Students' own answers.
3   Students' own answers.

Language focus

1

ominous

2

Late in the afternoon (it will be getting dark soon), stood for a moment against the sky, once well muscled, but now, for some reason, going to fat (we wonder why this might have happened), The fact that the two men are alone together in a quiet place makes the reader feel worried for the narrator, 'I haven't had a job that's lasted in forty years', he said (we wonder about the man's conduct – is he violent?) He sat down heavily, grunting (the man's physical strength is emphasized again), 'You'll be sorry you asked me to stay,' he said. 'Everyone always is.'

3

Sample answers:

1   light hearted, humorous (the description of the woman as a tabby cat is funny, and the reference to her purring is a humorous detail.)
2   reflective (the writer is looking back on his life. It is written in the present tense to reflect a life lesson he has learned.)
3   ominous, threatening (the words *desolate*, *fierce*, *roar*, *thundering* all suggest danger.)

4

Sample answer:

It was a beautiful place. I closed my eyes and listened to the gentle birdsong and the waves splashing below.

5

1	bare	3	skinny	5	tapped
2	gnarled	4	howled		

6

Sample answer:

This is a very good beginning for a short story because we meet the two main characters straight away. The Illustrated Man is immediately mysterious and the reader wants to know more about him. The mood is quickly established: we know that something bad is going to happen, and we want to read on to find out what it is.

7

Sample answer:

big, scary looking, ugly, sinister

The words from the text:

tall, once well muscled, going to fat, arms were long, hands thick, face was like a child's, set upon a massive body, wool shirt buttoned tight about his neck, his sleeves were rolled and buttoned down over his thick wrists, perspiration streaming from his face, heavily, grunting

8

| 1 | b | 2 | d | 3 | c | 4 | a |

9

| 1 | b | 2 | a | 3 | d | 4 | c |

10

1 b. The narrator meets the Illustrated Man one hot afternoon in the countryside.

2 a. The Illustrated man reveals his tattoos: the figures in his tattoos are alive and tell stories of the future.

3 d. The Illustrated man falls asleep. The narrator sees that one of the tattoos shows the Illustrated Man murdering him.

4 c. The narrator runs away from the Illustrated Man.

Get writing

1

Sample answer:

This is a tall, very thin woman in her early forties with brown bob-length hair. Her skin is pale and the skin under her eyes is lilac coloured. Her skin is unwrinkled apart from her brow which is furrowed. Her fists are usually clenched to hide her nails which are bitten and the skin on her fingers which is raw red. She smells of disinfectant and fabric softener. She always stands tall and her posture is very erect. She is well spoken.

2

Sample answer:

She scanned the crowds, shielding her eyes with one clenched hand. Paul and the little ones were nowhere to be seen amongst the thronging masses which jostled all around her. Craning her long neck to look down the platform she caught sight of her ghostly reflection in the mirror on the door. She instinctively straightened her back. Did she really look so old, so harassed? Wasn't this supposed to be a holiday?

3

Sample answer:

She scanned the crowds of relaxed and tanned holidaymakers, shielding her eyes from the sun's glare with one tightly-clenched fist. Paul and the little ones were nowhere to be seen, and yet the train was due to leave any minute. Craning her long neck to look down the platform, she caught sight of her ghostly reflection in the mirror on the door: a white and grim faced apparition among the suntanned youths who dotted the station, lying comfortably on their back packs as they waited for their trains. She remembered doing the same once and sighed at the memory. When had she begun to look so old, so weighed down by it all?

4

Sample answer:

There was still no sign of Paul and the children. The guard nodded to her as he walked past and muttered something in Catalan. They were going to miss their train. The children would cry and they would be left here, on the platform, in this sweltering heat with their enormous suitcase stuffed full of the clothes she had spent so long laundering and ironing before their departure. She watched as a group of teenagers skipped up the stairs and disappeared into a carriage, shouldering their backpacks with ease. Minutes later she saw them open the window and rest their bronzed elbows on the frame.

She would never know what force had drawn her off the platform and onto the train, but one thing she did know and it was this: from the inside of the train, the suitcase didn't look quite as big or as heavy as it had done before. She knew that Paul would be able to carry it, or else would be able to charm someone else to. He had, after all, always been a very charming man. As the train chugged out of the station there was still no sign of her family. She opened the window and let the warm fug of the August day caress her white hands.

Unit 16 Communicating emotion

Looking closely

1

1   The speech has been written to raise awareness of the damage that a large coffee shop chain is going to inflict on the local businesses and community life of a small town. The speaker wishes to motivate inhabitants of the small town to fight the coffee chain and protect local businesses.

2   The writer conveys disgust at the unfair methods of the coffee shop chain through word choice, describing the chain as 'bland, soulless and dull'. The writer also compares the coffee shop to a 'bully' in a 'playground'. In using inclusive language ('we can', 'join me') the writer makes the listeners feel involved in the struggle. Repetition ('The bully will not be ...') is also used to emphasise the speaker's point.

3   Yes, because the language is simple yet powerful. The writer includes the audience and uses emotive language to make listeners take the side of local businesses and want to fight the 'bully'. The text also displays passion but it is not angry or embittered – it is clear and thought-provoking.

Language focus

1

1   *bully* (repeated three times)

2   The speaker mentions the recent survey results.

3   Independent coffee shops are contrasted with a large coffee shop chain.

4   Frequent use of *you* and *we*; the writer thanks the audience for their presence; addresses audience as *fellow residents*.

5   The speaker jokes that the audience look energetic because they drink coffee at independent coffee retailers.

6   *bland, soulless and dull*

2

1   The repetition of *bully* emphasizes the underhand methods of the coffee chain, and helps to cement this image in the minds of the audience.

2   The concrete examples root the speech in fact.

3   The contrast of the 'bullying' coffee chain with the powerless independent coffee retailers is emotive – it makes the Café Co chain seem even more of a bully.

4   Direct address makes the audience feel included in the speech – they are part of the struggle.

5   The humour injects a positive note and relaxes the audience.

6   The list of three adjectives emphasizes the main point of the speech.

3

The Café co coffee shop chain is compared to a bully. It is much larger than the independent coffee shops and uses unfair, bullying methods to get what it wants, e.g. it *tramples* over its smaller competitors.

4

These emotive words are used to describe independent coffee shops and their supporters: *vitality, energy, energizing, quality, wonderful, nurtured, cherished*

These emotive words are used to describe the Café Co coffee chain: *bland, soulless, dull, mediocrity, bully, trampled, powerful*

The writers' use of emotive language helps to establish the large chain as cruel, ruthless and uninspiring. Meanwhile the independent shops are conveyed as creative and vibrant – they *nurture* rather than *trample*.

5

1   proud, joyful (a father of the bride speech)

2   Furious mobs, rioting (a political speech)

3   years of toil and hard graft (a graduation or retirement speech)

4   icy weather plunges our country into the coldest winter on record (a speech calling for volunteers)

5   the jewel in the crown (a speech at a marketing or tourism presentation)

6

1   Lottie and Leo are finally pledging their love for one another through marriage.

2   I would like to sincerely thank my teachers for their constant and unwavering support over the years.

3   My years spent in this department have been utterly rewarding, but all good things come to an end.

4   Thoughtless littering is the downfall of this town; its ugliness shadows our streets.

Looking closely

1

1   This is a wedding speech. It has been written by the sister of the bride.

2   The writer conveys the gratitude she feels to the wedding guests. Through the repetition of 'you have' she emphasizes the very important part that friends and family have played in the special day. The writer also emphasizes the strong emotions she herself feels on the day by using emotive words such as 'beautiful, lively and unforgettable'.

3   Yes, because it is warm, affectionate and suitably respectful to the bride, groom and wedding guests. However, it also contains sufficient humour to lighten the mood and make the guests feel relaxed.

Language focus

1

1   *You: You are the people … / You have honoured them by … / You have made this day …*

2   From the little girl who used to jump off walls dressed up as a butterfly, to the bigger girl who once decided to redecorate her bedroom using purple poster paints – Mum and Dad weren't too happy – my life with Vanessa has never been dull.

3   *from the little girl … to the bigger girl*

4   Many sentences begin with *You*

5   Humour is used throughout: from the opening joke about the camera to the humorous description of how Vanessa met her future husband.

6   *beautiful, lively and unforgettable; noise, hilarity and cheer; long, happy and eventful*

2

Repetition of *You* at the beginning of these sentences emphasizes the importance the speaker places on the guests and the part they have played in the wedding. Examples of Vanessa's exploits bring life to the speech and also provide humour. The contrast between *the little girl* and *the bigger girl* is also humorous as it shows that although Vanessa has grown up, she has remained the same in essence. Direct address throughout adds to the warmth and intimacy of this speech, while the humour prevents the speech from getting overly emotional and also relaxes the wedding guests. The lists of three adjectives add rhythm and emphasis to the speech.

3

honour, special, honoured, touched, generous, beautiful, lively, unforgettable, privileged, hilarity, cheer, hearts, wonderful, long, happy, eventful

The emotive words make the speech suitably moving and memorable for this important occasion.

Get writing

1

Sample answer:

I had put aside most of yesterday to write what I had planned to be a moving and eloquent speech. However, at ten o'clock my sister turned up at the door and urgently requested my presence at an impromptu picnic she had stuffed into a rucksack. When I mentioned the speech and the small matter of the wedding she had to organize, she just pointed to the sun streaming in through the window and told me to get a move on. As a result, this speech will be a little shorter and less eloquent than planned.

I tell you this story not to excuse the length of my speech, but to show you what I have always loved about Carrie – her love for life. It is impossible to be bored with Carrie around – her energy, vivacity and spontaneity make every occasion exciting. Life with my sister has always been unpredictable – my earliest memory of our time together is of me trying to persuade her not to do a handstand in the bath (I failed).

My sister has, it's true, made some pretty crazy decisions over the years. She also, occasionally, displays rare flashes of impeccable judgment and good taste. Her decision to marry Richard is, I'm sure you will agree, one such rare flash. I've never seen my sister so happy and I'm sure you will agree that they make a very special couple.

I'm sure you will all join me in wishing Carrie and Richard the happiest of futures together.

2

Sample answer:

When I started work in the French department here ten years ago, I felt nervous and ill at ease. How was I going to cope with the noise, backchat and wild behaviour? And that was just the teachers – how on earth was I going to deal with the pupils? I am happy to say that the feeling of nerves wore off as soon as I walked in the door. From the first day I started here I felt valued, supported and encouraged by all my teaching colleagues.

These ten years have gone too quickly. I will hold many memories of my time here close to my heart. The annual school trip to Paris, the end of term teacher shows and all the great laughs we have had over tea and biscuits together will never leave me.

As you know, my health is not what it used to be. I'd like to say a special thanks to those who have supported me over the past few months – you know who you are.

'They are able because they think they are able' – this is the motto of our school. This is the motto which is held dear by all you excellent teachers I've had the privilege of working with. This is the motto which you teach our students to hold in their hearts. And it is this motto which sums up my time here – to all of you who have helped me to believe in my own abilities as a teacher, please accept my sincere thanks.

3

Sample answer:

Friends and teachers. We are graduating. Can you believe it? Only four years ago we were just starting out on our learning journey here. Do you remember how wise and mature the older students appeared back then? Do you feel that wise and mature today?

It's been an amazing four years which has passed so quickly. The time has flown because of the inspiring lessons, wonderful social activities and supportive guidance we have experienced.

We all have so many positive memories of our time here – a good too many to list. Memories of school trips, end of year parties, sports days … I know I speak on behalf of every single one of us when I thank the teachers for their hard work, good humour and professionalism. It is you who make this college the welcoming and inspiring environment it is.

Well, today we head off into the world. Who knows what the future holds for us? Yet we can all be thankful for the sure start this college has granted us. This will help us take root, bloom and flourish wherever the wind may blow us.

4

Sample answer:

What is a home? Is it bricks, mortar and glass? Or is it where your heart is? You will all by now have heard of the council's plans for the new motorway. Is it right that the council are planning to bulldoze our houses for the sake of a new motorway?

Yes, this motorway might ease the congestion on the roads, but is that any substitute for the displacement of 83 people, half of whom are over the age of 70? How can we expect these people to rebuild their lives when the very heart has been ripped out of their community?

Residents of Fintry, stand up and let your voice be heard. The council's plan is senseless, cruel and short-sighted. The world does not need any more roads. What the world needs, and will always need, are close-knit communities. We, the people, will always need homes.

We can stop this if we unite against it. Join me in the fight against the proposed motorway today.

Unit 17   Adapting to different audiences

Looking closely

1

She is a young, successful Japanese artist. She had a happy childhood, and she lives in Hokkaido. She wants to study for a Masters in Fine Art in Boston. She also enjoys going to the cinema and shopping.

2

Text A: She has written about herself perhaps for an exhibition programme or her blog.

Text B: She is applying for a place on a Masters in Fine Art and has perhaps been asked to write a personal statement outlining her reasons for wanting to study this course.

Text C: She is probably living in Boston and finding it difficult to make friends. She is looking for people to socialise and get to know the city with.

Text D: She is writing this for pleasure and self-expression, perhaps in a creative writing class or as a blog entry to complement her visual art.

Language focus

1

Text A: Mayumi's professional biography is formal and is written in the third person. The biography is short and neutral in tone. Prospective employers or art buyers may read this biography, so the writing has to be professional.

Text B: Mayumi's autobiographical essay is written in the first person. It is formal, but some of the language is emotive, e.g. *passion, release*. Lecturers on the college selection panel will read this looking for evidence of commitment to the subject and prior achievements.

Text C: Mayumi's online profile is informal and chatty to appeal to other young people looking for friends.

Text D: Mayumi's memoirs are very descriptive and evocative. The tone is nostalgic: *I can still remember, we would* and she uses language to paint a picture of an idyllic time and place.

2

1   Text A

2   Text D

3   Texts B and D

4   Text A

5   Text C (Text A mentions free-time activities, but only those relevant to Mayumi's work.)

6   Text C

3

A   Professional and personal audience – amateur art lovers and professionals.

B   A formal application aimed at a university course coordinator.

C   A less formal audience – Mayumi is looking for new friends so she writers in a relaxed manner.

D   Mayumi wrote this piece for herself – she alone is the intended audience.

4

Mayumi has considered what each of her audiences would like/need to know. For example, the university she is applying to does not need to know about her interest in shoes and potential friends do not need a detailed work history or list of qualifications.

5

1   The sentence *He has a great sense of humour* could be rewritten to include a quirky hobby which demonstrates the writer's sense of humour, e.g. *When not writing or taking photographs, Jordan can be found chuckling loudly at Groucho Marx films.*

2   The sentence *Graduated with a degree in nursing five years ago* is probably not necessary. If the writer wants to emphasize his commitment to nursing, he could add an adjective, e.g. *Friendly, easy-going and committed nurse …*

3   The sentence *I also really enjoy flower arranging and meeting friends* is not necessary. The writer should keep the focus on astronomy.

6

Sample answers:

1   Geology has always fascinated me.

2   Her particular interest is second language acquisition.

3   If this sounds like you, let me know. Looking forward to meeting you!

7

Sample answers:

1   My six brothers and I spent our hungry-bellied childhoods in hand-me-down clothes and bare feet.

2   I am president of the University Social Programme Committee and divide my time between organizing fun student events and socializing with friends.

3   When I'm not hanging out with my mates, I love fancy-dress parties, football and comedy theatre.

4   In my final year of studying I took on extra courses in biology and Italian. I also helped to set up an online study forum for my year group.

Get writing

Sample answer:

1   Gabriella Zoican is an architect at Sun Life developments with a special interest in ecologically sustainable design. She has designed a series of solar-powered residential developments in the Bucharest area, and has won the coveted Green Europe award on two consecutive occasions. Gabriella's work has earned her accolades around Europe and in 2014 she was invited to present a paper at the International Architecture Conference in France.

Sample answer:

2   Hey, are you new to the city? Feeling lost and at a bit of a loose end? That makes two of us then – let's meet! Friendly, cheerful professional male seeks friends to go out and about with. Loves fine dining, films and chilling out at the weekend.

Sample answer:

3   I have enjoyed learning English for the past ten years. I have always looked for ways to improve, whether by eliciting feedback from teachers, attending extra communication sessions or by reading English-language novels and magazines. However, I now feel I have the time and energy to commit to a more intensive programme of study and it is for this reason that I am applying for a place on the Advanced Diploma in English Language. Having studied in a small school for many years, I would greatly appreciate the chance to discuss ideas with other English students.

Unit 18   Engaging your readers

Looking closely

1

British fashion, British sweets, the English language

2

c to reflect on her own experiences in the UK and entertain her readers. Cécile is writing this after one year of living in Britain – she refers to her *one-year anniversary*. She looks back on the things she found strange at first and compares her feelings then to her feelings now. She also wants to entertain her readers through the use of humour descriptive writing.

Language focus

1

Cécile's readers are probably people who are interested in British life. They may well be young like her and will probably be educated to a fairly high level – she touches on her learning experiences and her writing assumes a shared knowledge of learning a foreign language (the lingua franca *I needed to learn in order to succeed in life, Did I stand a slim chance (or even a fat chance) of succeeding in my studies?*

2

She invites comments – *It would be great to hear more suggestions about delights I have maybe yet to discover!*

3

affectionate

4

Cecile criticizes the dress sense and the lack of real croissants in the UK. Her criticisms are softened by the overall warm and affectionate tone of her piece.

5

1   gulp
2   constant torture
3   slim chance / fat chance (she is joking about the fact that both have a similar meaning.)

6

very critical

7

Sample answer:

This was only the beginning of what would be an interesting evening at 'The Hungry Beagle'. The house special was presented at our table with a flourish by our mysteriously taciturn waiter – a good ten minutes later I was still trying to work out what it was! Luckily, the carousel of sauces allowed me to add a little colour to the rather grey meal. Perhaps things might have picked up had we stayed for dessert. However, taking the prolonged absence of our waiter as a sign, we decided to call it a day.

8

1   The brackets divide the title of the post from its subtitle.
2   The brackets contain a humorous aside which contains extra information which is not essential to the overall meaning of the sentence.
3   The brackets contain a humorous aside.
4   The brackets contain clarification.
5   The brackets contain a humorous aside. This bracket also emphasizes the writer's point about English being a difficult language (both a *slim chance* and *a fat chance* mean a small likelihood of something happening).

9

This overuse of brackets makes the writer's prose disjointed and hard to follow.

10

After spending six fun-filled months in London, I decided it was high time to venture north and visit Scotland. I have always envisaged Scotland as a romantic land of myth, mist, castles and lakes, and wondered if the reality would live up to my dreams. Well, anyone who has ever arrived in Edinburgh (by train, anyway) will know that I was not disappointed.

The sight of Castle Rock, where Edinburgh Castle is located, filled me with excitement and anticipation about my stay.

11

1   It can be difficult to persuade my son (a complete computer fanatic) to leave the house.
2   It was Ellie (my personal trainer) who finally inspired me to kick the habit.
3   She clearly wanted to go home (not that I blamed her).
4   She's currently living in Skye (a beautiful island off the west coast of Scotland).
5   Vienna (or Becs as we call it in Hungarian) is my favourite European city.

Get writing

1

Sample answer:

I love Tuesdays! Our wonderful tutor generally keeps this afternoon free for communicative activities. Today we worked together to make a poster about entertainment possibilities in Edinburgh. After making our poster, we had to present our ideas to the rest of the class. I was a bit nervous, but once we got started I really enjoyed myself! We filmed our presentation, and you can view mine here.

For homework, we need to make a list of ideas for making suggestions about a town. If any of you lovely readers could submit your suggestions and help me with my homework, I'd be very grateful!

2

Sample answer:

3 top tips for learning new English words

When it comes to English vocabulary it can be difficult to know where to start. Here are my three top tips for learning (and remembering) new words:

1   For concrete nouns (e.g. *window sill, plant pot*), labelling items around your house really does work well. However, this technique is probably best if you live alone (parents can get pretty peeved if you start sticking bits of paper to their antique furniture).
2   When you come across a new word, try to use it at least five times every day for a week. Depending on the word you've learnt this can present some interesting challenges, but it does work!
3   Think carefully about how you group new words together in your vocabulary notebook. I have found that I remember words best when I group them in topics such as Family, Holidays, etc. but others may have different ideas.

If anyone out there has thoughts on how best to learn English vocabulary, please let me know – I'd love to hear from you!

3

Sample answer:

Top tips for budget travel

Times are hard, and if we want to travel, many of us will have to do it on the cheap. Here are some of my top budget tips:

1   Choose self-catering accommodation

One of the biggest expenses when travelling is eating out. Although enjoying local food is a travel highlight, choosing self-catering places means you can cook for yourself at least some of the time. Pasta is reliably cheap and filling, but not an option if you don't have a kitchen. Being able to make your own breakfast in the morning can take a good chunk off the cost of your holiday.

2   Travel overnight to save accommodation costs

Accommodation is another big cost, so why not combine it with travel? Last year I travelled in a sleeper compartment from Hungary to Istanbul. I enjoyed comfortable accommodation and amazing views at a fraction of what I would have paid for a flight and two nights in a hotel.

3   Mix business and pleasure

Why not consider a working holiday? You could teach, work at a summer camp or pick fruit – the possibilities are endless! Many employers throw in accommodation and food so you could be making money, saving money and enjoying a unique perspective of a new country all at the same time!

Any tips to add to the list, fellow budget travellers? I would love to hear your thoughts.

4

Sample answer:

I've had a few comments recently asking me to blog about the new French place which has opened up on Hanover Street. Well, yesterday was my birthday so I decided it was time to treat myself. Luckily I was not disappointed!

The first thing that struck me about *La Petite Deluge* was the rustic charm and simplicity of the decor. The second was the warm welcome we received from our charming waiter. My partner and I were offered a window seat which allowed us a wonderful opportunity to people watch and admire the amazing sunset.

The meal, when it arrived, was even better than I'd dared to hope. I had melt-in-the-mouth filo parcels of lamb marinated in pomegranate juice. Delicious! My partner was equally impressed with his duck paté. For our main course we both opted for the pan-fried chicken on a bed of black rice and celeriac. The meat was tender and the meal beautifully presented – my only small gripe was that the accompanying vegetables (roasted cherry tomatoes and peppers) arrived well into the meal.

This small complaint did nothing to detract from our overall satisfaction. I would strongly recommend *La Petite Deluge*. Book a table for tonight – you won't be disappointed!

Unit 19   Sharing news and information

Looking closely

1

Text A: raising awareness of a cause (site such as Facebook)

Text B: looking for help and advice in a professional context (site such as Twitter)

Text C: inviting friends to dinner (site such as Twitter)

Text D: sharing professional information (professional network such as LinkedIn).

Language focus

1

On the whole, the language is semi-formal / informal. Social media is a relatively relaxed arena, but it is still important to be clear and appropriate.

Semi-formal language: *Could you please say hello, It was good to catch up … , Educate yourself, educate others* and *take action.*

Informal language: *Hey, have u got that Friday feeling?, Fancy meeting up …*

2

1   B and C

2   D

3   B

4   C

5   All of them, especially B and C

6   D

7   A, B and D

3

1   The writer's friends.

2   The writer's friends/family.

3   The writer's peers/colleagues.

4   The writer's local community.

5   The writer of a blog / the readers of the blog.

4

No:

Sample answers:

1 The writer doesn't address any specific individual and doesn't sound very excited about the film.

2 The writer doesn't directly involve her readers.

3 The post is not sufficiently engaging or specific, so the writer is unlikely to get the help they need.

4 The post does not sound dramatic enough to prompt action.

5 The writer has misspelt several words.

5

Sample answers:

1 @nsimes Fancy the new Bond film tonight? Got fab reviews: Bit.ly.le6.gh

2 Looking for a great meal? Check out *Little Venice* for delicious lasagne. Here's a pic!

3 Wanted: students to answer questions about their use of Facebook. Send a DM if interested and please RT. Bit.ly.me6.vr

4 Save our library! Love books? Please help by signing our petition now!

5 Fascinating post, as usual, Karl. I totally agree with your point about air pollution – we have to do something quickly – the government cannot be trusted to act on our behalf.

Looking closely

1

1 True

2 True

3 False. Use active verbs wherever possible.

4 True

5 False. This will make it look like you are shouting.

2

1 c   2 d   3 a   4 b

Language focus

1

She is trying to promote her restaurant.

2

Her posts are very short and make no attempt to engage her readers. She uses confusing text speak and abbreviations. She makes little attempt to sell her restaurant or show how it is different from the other restaurants in town.

3

Sample answers:

1 Another happy customer review "Just had the best king crab noodles ever"

2 We have so many kinds of noodles you'd be off your noodle not to try us! Happy Hour all day!

3 Forget your money worries with today's meal deal. Buy 1 chicken & rice, and get 1 free!

4 Thanks Mum! Lunch today is on us for all Mums. #HappyMothersDay

Get writing

1

Sample answer:

Got a special day coming up? We offer custom-made cakes for all occasions!

We should all eat more vegetables! Try our oven-fresh carrot cake.

What's your favourite cake? Tell us and we'll bake it on our Friday requests day.

Crumbs, thanks! "The new cake shop on Main St is awesome!"

Check out this fab banana loaf recipe: bit.ly/m2TV6

2

Sample answer:

Get on your bike! National Bike to Work Week hits Aberdeen this week: make sure you're ready! Post your cycling photos on Facebook and tell your friends how fantastic cycling feels.

3

Sample answer:

I'm just back from a stimulating training weekend in London. The theme: business lessons we can learn from global neighbours. My personal highlight was a convivial workshop led by renowned entrepreneur Ron Pretty. Ron led us through a range of discussion exercises and role-play activities: you can see a short clip of the work we produced here. A great weekend of networking and exchanging ideas!

4

Sample answer:

Do you run a small business in the London area? Would you like the opportunity to meet and network with other small businesses? Then come to a one day networking event at 'The Innovation Suite' 35 Holloway Road on the 23rd April. Browse titles at our business fair, engage in workshops led by business professionals and be inspired! The proceedings start at 10 a.m. and will finish at 5 p.m. This event is always popular so click here to book early!

Unit 20   Writing notes

Looking closely

1

1   Lucy has attended a lecture on the different way in which mushrooms can save the world.

2   Lucy has not attempted to write down every word the lecturer says. For example, instead of transcribing questions in full she writes a question mark beside an abbreviated sentence, e.g. *poss. solution 2 energy crisis?* She uses dashes to link ideas, and she also uses abbreviations.

Language focus

1

mshrm (mushroom), sat (saturated), dstryd (destroyed), b (be), 2 (to), Grp (group), Exp (experience), hrs (hours), x (times), nat. (natural), exp. (experiments), bcome (become), trt (treat), poss (possible)

2

1	c	3	h	5	a	7	f
2	d	4	g	6	e	8	b

3

Sample answers:

1   Early chldhod ed. creates better jobs & cn ∴ prmte stronger ecnmy.

2   Microbes on ur skin can help boost ur immune system – microbes in mouth freshen breath.

3   In rcnt yrs the profile of rfgs has chngd – r younger, move with fam. & emgrte 4 £ reasons.

Looking closely

1

1

Advantages: This is a straightforward way of noting the most important points in the order you hear them.

Disadvantages: This method does not make it so easy for the writer to draw connections between ideas.

2

Advantages: Making notes in columns with headings makes it is very easy to read and find the relevant information when you revisit your notes.

Disadvantages: We don't always know in advance what different topics (or sub-topics) we are going to hear about in a lecture so this method is not always possible.

3

Advantages: Spidergrams allow you to see the connections between ideas. They can also easily be added to at any time as you learn more about a topic.

Disadvantages: Spidergrams can get very messy, and can be difficult to decipher later on. They are not much use if you need to write a lengthy explanation.

Language focus

1

Sample answers:

1   The outline method would be effective if you were reading about someone's life and times, as this kind of text is likely to tackle points in a sequential manner.

2   You could use a spider diagram. Write the word *Creativity* in the middle of the page, and then make connections between ideas using arrows.

3   You could use a table strategy with the causes as your headings, and notes on each underneath.

Get writing

Sample answer:

1   The outline strategy would be a good one to try. Alternatively, the Cornell strategy allows you to clearly record key words (e.g. names of scientists and scientific discoveries) so this would work well here too.

2   Students' own answers.

3   Students' own answers.

ACKNOWLEDGEMENTS

The Publisher and author wish to thank the following rights holders for the use of copyright material:

Unit 3

Dogs in parks: proposed restrictions

Adapted extract from www.harringayonline.com/forum/topics/dogs-in-parks-proposed-restrictions reproduced by permission of Harringay Online

Unit 7

Article name: 'Lean-In' and the Era of the Inconvenienced Mom

Author: Leonore Skenazy

This article appeared in the 24 March 2013 edition of The Wall Street Journal

http://online.wsj.com/article/SB10001424127 8873234153045783710115786671052.html reproduced by permission of Dow Jones & Company, Inc. All rights Reserved Worldwide

Unit 15

Extract from *The Illustrated Man* by Ray Bradbury (2008) 978-0-00-647922-2 reproduced by permission of HarperCollins Publishers Ltd

Unit 19

Twitter images, design and content:

Twitter, Inc for the use of the Twitter logo and text from www.twitter.com

The Publisher also wishes to acknowledge the following source used for information when writing articles:

Unit 4

Comments on a travel blog

http://my.englishclub.com/profiles/blogs/is-tourism-good-or-bad-for

---

Photo credits

All images are from Shutterstock.

Cover: michaeljung; p8: Kzenon; p12: elena moiseeva; p16: Hasloo Group Production Studio, Hasloo Group Production Studio, pattyphotoart, Zurijeta; p18: solominviktor, Oleg Mikhaylov, Ariwasabi, solominviktor; p20: Rido; p22: Masson, c12, project1photography, Hans Kim; p24: Dragon Images; p28: Champion studio; p32: Rob Marmion; p36: wavebreakmedia, Joerg Beuge; p40: Goodluz; p44: zimmytws; p48: Goodluz; p52: racorn; p56: auremar; p60: Valua Vitaly, Fesus Robert; p64: Mila Supinskaya; p68: Anatolii Riepin; p72: takayuki, NH; p73: takayuki; p76: Lucky Business, QQ7; p80: Kzenon; p82: Lee319; p84: wavebreakmedia.

If any copyright holders have been omitted, please contact the Publisher who will make the necessary arrangements at the first opportunity

Collins Also available

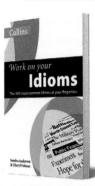